Hollywood the Hard Way, A Cowboy's Journey

A true tale of adventure

by

Patti Dickinson

Bitterroot Mountain Publishing
Hayden, Idaho 83835

Visit our Website www.BitterrootMountainPublishing.com

First Edition
10 9 8 7 6 5 4 3 2

ISBN: 978-0-9852784-2-7 (eBook)
ISBN: 978-1-940025-19-3 (Trade Paperback)

Cover design by Larry Telles

Print layout by eBooks By Barb for booknook.biz

Also By Patti Dickinson

**Coach Tommy Thompson
And the Boys of Sequoyah**

The Indian's Daughter

The Fifth Season

Courage is the not the absence of fear, but the conquest of it.

Anonymous

Contents

Acknowledgements

The story of Jerry Van Meter's journey could easily have been lost were it not for the strength of oral history and the cooperation of many helpful people. Though they are gone now, Elizabeth Eaton Wise, Frank "Pistol Pete" Eaton's daughter, and Linda Lee Wakely, Jimmy Wakely's daughter, sharing their pictures and stories and anecdotes let us get to know their famous fathers. The thorough genealogical work of the late Lee Goodnight aided greatly in capturing the spirit and the character of cattle baron Charles Goodnight. Thankfully, Elizabeth, Linda, and Lee all got the opportunity to read *Hollywood the Hard Way* and recognize their contribution to the story.

Jerry Van Meter's brothers, James, David, William, and Byron deserve infinite thanks for their contributions. Each one's heartwarming, poignant reminiscences of the Van Meter and Goodnight families is what formed the heart and soul of this story.

Sincere appreciation to Dr. Brad Agnew, outstanding author and professor of History at Northeastern State University in Tahlequah, Oklahoma for his contribution and insight into Oklahoma's war years. Equally appreciated are the efforts of John Fusco, writer, director, and producer of the movie *Hidalgo,* for his equine knowledge and expertise in proving that Jerry's Osage Indian mare, Fan, possessed the endurance traits to complete such an arduous journey. Thanks also to Captain (retired) Kenneth Myatt of the California Highway Patrol for his active participation and painstaking research into the history of the CHP.

My heartfelt thanks to Julie Woody, former waitress in that Montana cowboy bar, for sitting down at my table and telling me, "boy do I have a story you have to write." I am grateful for that chance encounter for it launched me on a wonderful journey of my own.

Lastly, I want to thank my husband David for his support and enthusiasm, and for embracing my steadfast commitment to tell this amazing story.

Introduction

I first heard this story in a little restaurant/bar on the shores of Flathead Lake in western Montana. It was lunchtime, the bar was across the highway from my motel, and the writer's conference I planned to attend wasn't due to start for another hour. Dressed professionally for the seminar in a suit and high heels, I walked over to the bar, noting the *This is Bud Country* neon sign in the window. The sign did give me pause, but I entered anyway. A glance around the smoky interior revealed that the only patrons were cowboys! All conversations stopped and there was dead silence as every Stetson-topped head turned my way, surprise registered on every face.

I froze, seriously considering a hasty retreat but just then a tall, slender waitress came out from behind the bar; she smiled as she gave me the once-over. "You are obviously lost, can I help you?" Already embarrassed, it seemed a bit late to back down now, so I sat down at a table, ordered a beer and the *Montana Burger,* and tried my best to look nonchalant. The waitress's obvious amusement, however, did prompt me to tell her about the writers' conference nearby. "Oh, now I understand. So, you are a writer?" she said, her expression changing to interested.

When I answered, "Yes I am," the waitress introduced herself as Julie Woody and said she would be back in a few minutes. True to her word, she soon returned with my lunch. Julie then surprised me by pulling out a chair and sitting down at my table. "Boy, do I have a story you have to write," she said and launched into a tale about a young cowboy, who, in 1946 to honor a bet his grandfather made with a famous movie star, rode his horse 1,500 miles from Guthrie, Oklahoma to Hollywood. "But in order to win the bet, he had to get there in fifty days!"

At hearing the word Oklahoma, my home state, Julie now had my undivided attention. The cowboy, her father's age now, attended their same church and in a casual conversation with her dad one Sunday, had mentioned his ride. The more she talked about the cowboy's journey, the more it reminded me of the stories I grew up hearing about my gun-toting, half-Cherokee grandfather; exciting wild-west tales of his early life in Oklahoma.

It didn't take her long to relate what she knew, but in those few minutes Julie hooked me like a prize catch from the lake's pristine waters. Something clicked, and I experienced a rush of feelings that my stopping in this unlikely place (for me) was not just happenstance after all. And just maybe, I was meant to write this story. My reaction? I *had* to meet this cowboy and find out the details of his ride. At the end of my lunch I made Julie a promise. "If what you told me is true, I *will* write that story."

Heroes exist. Disasters highlight their deeds and we see them briefly on the evening news. But rarely do we get to know them, the everyday person who lifts himself or herself above the crowd by accomplishing an extraordinary feat. If the man actually did what Julie said, I had a hero in my sights, at least a hero by my definition.

It didn't take me long to discover where Jerry Van Meter lived, but as luck would have it, he and his wife had just left to Arizona for the winter. So for the next five months, I periodically checked with Julie and the following spring heard the good news that the Van Meters were back in Montana. The bad news, Jerry was in a Kalispell hospital with serious heart problems. Not about to give up, I kept checking on him. All told, it took me thirty phone calls over twelve months to finally get an interview with my potential hero. Perseverance pays!

Ironically, our first meeting took place on September 19, 1995, exactly one year to the day that I first heard his story in the cowboy bar. A handsome, silver-haired gentleman with a ready smile, Jerry greeted me politely in his gentle Oklahoma accent. I told him what little of the story I'd heard and asked if it were true. He nodded, "Yes it is." After a year of waiting I had my answer, albeit brief. I asked him to tell me a little about the journey and Jerry obliged as he unfolded a worn map. He touched the stub of a pencil to his tongue and started tracing a path across the yellowed paper, his blue eyes mirroring excitement as he talked. It was as if his ride had taken place yesterday instead of more than sixty years ago. I listened in amazement but finally managed to ask, "That sounds like one heck of a ride—was it?" I had waited an entire year to hear his answer.

"It was sure something, all right," Jerry said. Not exactly the description I had hoped to hear, but my excitement returned when he began to describe some of the country he rode through and the people he encountered. When Jerry got to the *why* of his ride and the famous names responsible for him taking it, it hit me that I had just uncovered a precious piece of Americana history. I silently blessed Julie and thanked Providence for not making a fast exit from the bar. Surprised that I (or anyone) would think his journey was worth writing about, Jerry finally agreed to let me tell his story.

I lived in Coeur d'Alene, Idaho at the time so once a month for the following year I made the four hundred-mile roundtrip drive to Kalispell, Montana and taped lengthy interviews with Jerry. In between visits, I telephoned him almost every day with a list of questions, which he graciously answered. His keen recollection of places and names impressed and delighted me, but as I began to transcribe the tapes, the daunting scope of his story began to emerge. It dented my confidence, but not my resolve.

The challenge to bring the towns to life and accurately portray them and the landscape as it was in 1946, took another twelve months of research. It required studying history books of that era, pouring over old maps, and delving into city and state records. Thankfully, most of the newspapers from the towns Jerry rode through had digitally archived old issues. For a nominal fee, I was able to get photo copies of specific dates. Admittedly a painstaking effort, but it revealed noteworthy headlines of the day and poignant stories—intimate glimpses into history.

Two years after our first meeting, with a bare-bones draft of Jerry's ride, it was retracing a good part of his route (in the comfort of an air conditioned car) that solidified my initial impressions. This indeed was a story worth telling. The trip reinforced my awe and admiration of a twenty-year-old cowboy's incredible feat. One man, one horse, fifteen hundred miles over some of the toughest terrain in our country simply to win a bet his grandpa made.

Surprisingly, half a century later some of the towns were little-changed, such as Magdalena, Pie Town, and Quemado in New Mexico. The Apache trading post in Cibecue, Arizona, and farther west, Quartzsite, Arizona looked exactly the way Jerry described them.

An abundance of lengthy interviews with Jerry's four brothers and other members of his family enabled me to recreate the scenes and dialogue that led to his journey and to show Oklahoma as it was in 1945-46. Most of the incidents and conversations of that time, Jerry remembered. Still, the passage of sixty-plus years could not help but fade *some* memories, requiring literary license in the few instances of incomplete data or conflicting accounts.

Every attempt has been made to relay the truth, for it is in the truth that the simple beauty of this story lies.

By the early 1890s, Oklahoma was divided roughly in half between Oklahoma Territory and Indian Territory, a raw land not yet part of the Union. Children of that era grew up on stories about Indians, gunfighters, cowboys, cattle drives, and great land runs. By the time Oklahoma became a state in 1907, most of those youngsters were grown and had children of their own. They passed these stories on to their sons and daughters, a generation that came of age in the late 1920s, just two years shy of the onset of the Great Depression.

The Dust Bowl and Depression years and their impact on Oklahomans have been chronicled in countless books. But it is the unforgettable images in the 1939 film *The Grapes and Wrath* based on John Steinbeck's novel that gave us the visual symbols of the darkest period in Oklahoma history. The men, women, and children who lived through those epochal years comprised the robust generation that energized the era that followed. It is important to note here, that it would be another ten years before Oklahoma's non-English speaking Native Americans would feel any measurable relief from the devastating poverty of the Great Depression.

The war years, 1941-45, became a boom-time in Oklahoma, the forties decade delivering the state and most of its citizens from the Depression's economic stranglehold. Government dollars, under the umbrella of defense spending, flowed into the state, employing thousands of men and women hungry for jobs. Contractors and construction companies built military bases and aeronautical schools. Oklahoma factories turned out fighter and cargo planes, as well as medium and heavy bombers.

Federal money funded training programs for pilots, bomber crews, and other critical flight personnel. It turned thousands of acres of farmland into a military city—Camp Gruber, larger than many Oklahoma towns, and so well equipped that several divisions could all train at the same time. Ammunition, explosives, tanks, planes, bombs, and armored vehicles, it can be said that almost every component needed to conduct the war could be traced to Oklahoma. And under the pressure of "national emergency," every endeavor, no matter the size, was completed at lightning-fast speed.

Despite the impact of this pivotal decade, at World War II's end in 1945, farming still involved half of the state's population. Imbued with a rich history of the past, this generation became part of Oklahoma's postwar revival, blending industrialism with a pioneer spirit reflective of the nineteenth century.

Like Route 66, that magical stretch of highway that linked Chicago to Los Angeles, postwar Oklahoma incorporated the best of the old world and the new, with citizens who well-remembered their history but embraced the future with open arms.

Oklahomans born in the 1920s and came of age in the 1940s formed a new generation. They revered their grandparents who had arrived in the Territory on horseback or in a prairie schooner, but realized that their own dreams were tied to the postwar future. They comprised a vibrant generation with a pioneer past, a promising future, and one foot solidly in each world.

What follows is the adventure of one such young man. This is the story he told me.

– 1 –

Mr. Hollywood

Enid Morning News September 17, 1945
• *Thousands Line Enid Streets For Colorful Parade* •
• *Jimmy Wakely, Monogram Star, Heads Cherokee Strip Entertainment* •
• *Goodnight And Eaton End Chisholm Trail Ride To Kick Off*
52nd Annual Festival •

Jerry Van Meter let Buster have free rein. The quarter horse knew the trails around the Bar R Ranch as well as its rider. Jerry never tired of this countryside, the rolling hills, the creeks that snaked their way across the Oklahoma prairie, the wind-shaped trees that dotted the horizon. All were as familiar as his own reflection. Family roots, cherished memories, and generations of stories made this landscape home.

Bright after the night's storm, the moonlight danced across the top of fields of golden grass bent by the breeze. Crickets, cicadas, coyotes, and lowing cattle filled the air with their sounds. Departing clouds scurried southeast toward Arkansas, scattering life-giving rain as they went. Up ahead, porch lights from the ranch house sent pale slivers of light out across the yard.

The Bar R's five thousand acres sat smack in the middle of the prairie between Enid and Marshall in northwest Oklahoma. Home to Jerry and his grandfather, Rolla Goodnight, the ranch also contained a dozen or so draft and quarter horses, two or three milk cows, numerous cats, dogs, and chickens, eight hundred head of Herefords, and five ranch hands. And a good part of the time, Rolla's life-long friend, Frank "Pistol Pete" Eaton, lived there as well. Everyone said that even a blind man could follow the trail between Frank's home in nearby Perkins and the Bar R.

As he neared the house, Jerry spotted Frank's oversized cowboy hat and Rolla's six feet, two inch frame silhouetted against the house's white siding. The two of them were talking to someone. Buster slowed to a walk and took his own sweet time getting to the gate, finally stopping in front of the house. Jerry recognized the third figure as Jimmy Wakely, another long-time friend of his grandfather's.

Jimmy Wakely, Hollywood movie cowboy and Monogram Pictures star, along with his band had been the main entertainment at the huge Fifty-Second Annual Cherokee Strip Celebration. The three days of festivities held in Enid in mid-September every year commemorated the 1893 Oklahoma land rush that led to pioneers homesteading more than six and a half million acres of former Cherokee tribal hunting grounds. Earlier in the day, Wakely had ridden his movie horse, Lucky, at the head of the biggest parade in Enid's history.

But the movie cowboy had traded his fancy cowboy clothes for faded jeans and shirt and scuffed boots. Wakely rose as Jerry walked up on the porch. "Nice to see you, Jerry. You've sure grown up since I last saw you."

Jerry agreed with what he'd heard during the celebration; that Jimmy Wakely and Bing Crosby looked like brothers. They were of similar height and build, with the same handsome face and smooth crooner voice. At Saturday night's dance Jimmy had brought the house down singing *You Can't Break the Chains of Love*, his latest Decca release. Jerry decided Wakely fit in well with the folks of Enid; he had invited everyone in his easy "I'm just one of you folks" way to see *Saddle Serenade*, his latest movie due out in two weeks. The appreciative crowd kept him singing on stage for another half hour.

"Your granddad invited me to spend my last night in Oklahoma at a real cattle ranch," Jimmy said and offered his hand.

"Glad you could make it, Mr. Wakely." Jerry shook his hand.

"Sure enjoyed your music at the dance. I didn't think the crowd was ever going to let you quit."

"Call me Jimmy, would you? Mister sounds too formal. Rolla tells me you're the foreman here at the Bar R."

"Yes, sir."

Wakely smiled. "Sir. That's right. You were in the service, weren't you? What branch?"

"The Navy," Jerry said softly and looked down at his boots. "Not very long though. I ah...I didn't get to fin..." Jerry glanced at his grandfather. "I wasn't in there long enough to do any good."

"Well, no need to call me sir either, Jerry. Just plain old Jimmy will do."

Jerry straightened up and looked at Wakely. "Okay, Jimmy it is. I'd better take care of Buster and get to bed. After camping out on the Chisholm Trail for two weeks with these guys, then celebrating for three days in town, my work is stacked up. Tomorrow's gonna be a big day." Jerry gathered up Buster's reins and started for the barn.

Jimmy called after him. "My horse, Lucky, is in the barn. Would you mind checking on him when you take care of Buster?"

"Be glad to. 'Night, everybody."

Rolla, Jerry (kneeling) Frank, and Fan on the Chisholm Trail, September 1945,
Photo courtesy of Jerry Van Meter

Jimmy Wakely on Lucky, his movie horse, circa 1945.
Photo courtesy of Lindalee Wakely

– 2 –

Better See if Hell's Froze Over

Enid Daily Eagle, September 17, 1945
• *Storm Drops .38" Of Rain, Drought Continues* •
• *Eisenhower Promises 2.4 Million Troops Home By Christmas* •
• *Millions of Vets Expected To Apply For Funds Under New G I Bill* •

Rolla watched as his grandson disappeared into the barn. Neither Jimmy nor Frank had noticed Jerry's embarrassment at the mention of the navy. Yet every time the subject of being in the service came up, Jerry reacted the same way, embarrassed and ashamed. Rolla could not forget Jerry's arrival at the Bar R right after his discharge; the shock of seeing him that way still hurt. He returned in the dead of winter, thin and drawn and pale as a ghost. Sweat had broken out on his forehead when he struggled to walk up the three steps to the porch and into the house. Trussed in a back brace and obviously in great pain, he briefly glanced at his grandfather. "From a baseball game," Jerry half-whispered, then never spoke of it again.

A gust of wind rattled the porch windows. Rolla pushed the memory from his mind and breathed deep the earth's damp fragrance. The autumn evening, interrupted by a fast-moving rainstorm, had given way to air crackling with freshness. Rain clung to the leaves of the big cottonwood near the house, drops shimmering like twinkling Christmas lights.

Wakely sighed. "Mmmh, you can't buy a perfume as good as the prairie right after a rain." He closed his eyes and smiled. "Plus I can still smell a little bit of that fried chicken. You and Frank did a good job on supper. That's the best meal I've had since I left California." A coyote howled in the distance and was soon joined by a chorus. "And I haven't heard coyotes that weren't part of a script in a coon's age. This is heaven, you know that?" Jimmy said, slapping at insects that buzzed around him.

"Won't argue with that," Rolla said. "I feel sorry for you, having to go back to California tomorrow."

"Right this minute, so do I. It's good to be back home. These folks are sure salt of the earth people."

"They love you, that's for sure," Frank said.

"That's because they think I'm a real cowboy. They're confusing what they see on the screen with guys like you." Wakely drained his glass of iced tea and gestured at the moonlit vista. "What a beautiful sight. Too bad it's disappearing."

Rolla glanced at Jimmy, expecting to see a smile accompany the joke. "What do you mean? What's disappearing?"

"Ranches like this, dyed-in-the-wool cowboys like you two. This whole way of life," Jimmy said.

Surprise registered on Frank's lined face. "Whoa, partner. You're joshin', right?"

"No, Frank, I wish I were," Jimmy said with a shake of his head. "The days of cattle barons like Charlie Goodnight are long-gone, so are the days of cowhands driving big herds thousands of miles. The only way you're going to see that anymore is in the movies." Wakely poured himself another glass of tea from the pitcher next to his chair. "Like *Cheyenne Roundup* and *The Old Chisholm Trail* that I made with Johnny Mack Brown and Tex Ritter, remember?"

"Yeah, but—" Frank's brow furrowed.

"They're all we have left to show what those days were like. I'm sorry to say, but I believe your way of life at the Bar R is going the same way." Wakely turned to Rolla. "Can you name me one cattleman today in Oklahoma or Texas, who is anything like your cousin, Charlie Goodnight?"

Rolla thought for a moment. "Well…not right off hand," he said, rubbing his chin. "I'll admit men were a might different in the old days. Charlie was a renegade, reckless as all get out, but smarter 'n a whip. He was to cattle in the 1800s what Frank Phillips is to oil in the 1900s." Rolla pictured Charlie and chuckled. "He loved to joke. One time somebody took his photograph standing by a buffalo, their heads right close together. When he saw the picture, he cussed up a blue streak, the gist of which was that the damn buffalo was near as good looking as him. Charlie taught me everything I know about the cattle business," Rolla said. "I never would have hung onto the Bar R and made it through the Depression if it wasn't for him. I used everything he taught me."

Jerry called out from the dimly lit bunkhouse across the yard. "Lucky seems right at home, Jimmy. See y'all in the morning."

Rolla acknowledged his grandson with a wave. He turned to Jimmy. "When I was fourteen, I left my folks in Kansas and rode pert' near three hundred miles to the Palo Duro, Charlie's ranch in the Texas Panhandle. I wanted to be a cowboy like him. And he taught me good. Being a rancher and a cowboy is all I know. If what you're saying is true, what's that say about my life? And Frank's too."

"It says you and Frank are a special breed of men—which you damn sure are—and that you've lived a period of history that won't ever be again." Jimmy pointed at the landscape. "This country is changing fast now that the war is over. My band and I travel all over, so I see it. Big change. Soldiers already home are getting married and moving to cities so they can go to college under the new G. I. Bill. Building is booming, families selling their farms right and left and moving to the city. And this is just the beginning."

"The beginning of what?" Frank said.

"The future, Frank. Seems like the United States is beginning to wake up from a long sleep—first the Depression then four years of sacrifice waiting until we finished with the war. Now that it's over, people don't want things to go back to the way they were. They want a better life. I'm telling you, when the rest of the troops get home, they're going to do the same thing—kiss farm life goodbye and move to Oklahoma City, Tulsa, or Muskogee. They're going to get factory jobs, maybe build a house and buy a new car. It's already happening in California. People are flocking into L.A.—all of southern California, like moths to a flame. Cities everywhere are exploding overnight." Jimmy's expression, at first grim, turned to a smile. "I hate to be the one to break the news to you, but before long it's going to happen here, too. Then you'll have to go to the theater in Enid and pay money to see me or Gene Autry or Roy Rogers doing the stuff you've been doing all your life."

Frank gazed at Wakely, his amusement barely concealed. "Funny, you got a smile on your face, but you don't sound like you're joshin'."

An Australian Shepherd appeared out of the darkness, ambled up on the porch and settled down at Rolla's feet. "I got a crew of five good young cowboys," Rolla said. "I don't see them hoppin' up and down to leave."

Wakely reached over and scratched the dog's neck. "You know as well as I do they're not near the caliber cowboy you and Frank are." Rolla wanted very much to dismiss what Jimmy said, but he knew better. At least once a month the Enid or Guthrie papers carried a story about Jimmy Wakely and his band playing in some city around the country. *He's in a better position than me to see change taking place. And Jimmy's not one to say something important like that if he didn't believe it.* Rolla suddenly wished their conversation hadn't taken this turn; it gave him an uneasy feeling.

Jimmy insisted. "Be honest now. Are you telling me your cowboys would know how to pull a cow out of quicksand or stop a stampede in the middle of a norther'? Could they stand eating beans and bacon three meals a day for three months? You know very well they couldn't. And not a one of them could sit in the saddle for fifteen hundred miles like you guys did."

"You paint a sorry picture, Jimmy, but when you talk *cowboy*, you're talking Charlie Goodnight. One of a kind, that man," Frank said, his handlebar mustache shifting angles as he spoke. "Always thunderin' around on them bow legs, cussin' up a storm. He could cuss better 'n any man I ever knew. 'Course when you own a million acres and run a hundred thousand head of cattle on your ranch, you can purty much talk like you want."

"I didn't know you knew him, Frank," Wakely said.

"I surely did. My uncle, Nick Eaton, had a spread on Running Water Creek in Texas. He and Charlie was friends. Remember, Rolla, that time we rode with Nick and Charlie and Deaf Smith to Caldwell, Kansas? Charlie rode right alongside, wrangling like one of us. He was a tough old bugger. I run across lots of men in my time—lawmen, good Indians, bad Indians, and a whole passel of gunfighters 'n thieves. Colt Younger and his bunch and Belle Starr, I knew all of them. Every one of 'em robbed for a livin', even Belle. You couldn't call one of them a legend, except for Pat Garrett. He was the finest lawman I ever run into. Killed Billy the Kid, you know. But Charlie Goodnight, now we're talkin' legend. Yessiree. The things I learned from him saved my hide more than once."

Lightning flashed in the distance, its retreating light illuminating the contour of the prairie. Frank went into the house and came out with three mugs of coffee. He handed one to Rolla and another to Jimmy.

"Thanks," Jimmy said. "*You* lived with him, Rolla, what was Charlie like? I've read about some of the things he did, but what kind of man was he?"

Rolla sipped his coffee thoughtfully. "Fearless. Charlie wasn't afraid of nothing or nobody. He was a Texas Ranger when he was young. And Charlie never got tired like an ordinary man. Even as a kid I had a hard time keeping up with him. He was a cattleman through and through. That's all he thought about. He ate, drank, and slept cattle. When we weren't riding, he'd read about cattle or talk to me about the cattle business, always trying to improve the herd. And

Charlie was as practical as they come. You know those chuck wagons you use in the movies?"

Wakely smiled. "Sure. They come with a cantankerous cook like Gabby Hayes who dishes out make-believe grub and medicine, and gives advice whether you want it or not."

"Well, it was ever-practical Charlie Goodnight that invented the chuck wagon. He took a military supply wagon, changed it around some and equipped it for cookin' so they could use it on long cattle drives."

"Well, I never knew that," Jimmy said.

"I ain't sure we'll ever see a man like him again," Frank said and then downed the last of his coffee.

Rolla raised his mug in a toast. "Charlie Goodnight was bigger than life: tough, bull-headed, always ready for adventure. He loved ranchin' more 'n anything. I'm proud to say I'm part of that tradition. It's something I'd like to pass on to my grandson. I'm not crazy about hearing the way of life I've spent seventy-five years livin' is damned near gone."

"I said I didn't like being the one to tell you." Jimmy shrugged.

"Wait a minute, mister. Are you saying cowboyin' is dead all together?" Frank said. The dog raised his head at Frank's sharp voice.

"Not just cowboyin', Frank," Jimmy said. He gestured at the Bar R. "I'm talking family ranching and this whole way of life. There just aren't any men around like you two anymore."

Frank stood up and pointed his gnarled finger at Jimmy. "Nosiree bob! People are always gonna eat steak. Steak don't grow on trees so runnin' cattle means you need horses. Horses have to have cowboys ridin' 'em and that ain't gonna change! That's all I got to say." Muttering something about needing more coffee, Frank disappeared into the house with a slap of the screen door.

Rolla decided he'd heard enough. "Now you listen, Mr. Holly-wood. I got somebody working for me that's as good a cowboy as me 'n Frank ever was. My grandson, Jerry, he can ride from here to hell and gone, break a horse, ride a bull, and rope a cow with the best of 'em."

Frank returned with the coffee pot and started to fill Rolla's mug. "Hold that danged thing still or I'm gonna pour this down your boot," he said. Frank refilled their mugs and set down the pot. "I heard what Rolla said about Jerry and he's right. Old-time cowboys like us got nothin' on that boy."

Wakely laughed. "Glory be, Rolla Goodnight and Frank Eaton agreeing on something? You're only saying that because he's your grandson, Rolla. Jerry's young. I don't see how he could be *that* good."

Rolla stood up to his full height, punctuating the air with his forefinger as he spoke. "I am not saying it because he's my grandson. I am saying it because it's the truth," he said hotly. "You don't know what that boy's been through. He's tough as they come. And not only that, he's got Goodnight blood runnin' in his veins. He learned cowboyin' from Frank 'n me from the time he could walk. Why, he took to it like a duck to water. Jerry is a cowboy clean through." Rolla leaned over, locking eyes with Jimmy, his voice measured. "I am willing to put my money where my mouth is. Are you?"

"Hot damn, I'm likin' this now." Frank said, slapping his thigh.

Wakely whistled. "I can't believe it, a Goodnight making a bet? I'd better check to see if hell's froze over." Jimmy was still chuckling as he and Rolla shook hands. "What kinda money are we talking about, Rolla?"

Rolla Goodnight and Frank Eaton as young men, 1886.
Photo Courtesy of Elizabeth Eaton Wise

Jerry Van Meter, age 16, at Guthrie farm with his model planes.
Photo courtesy of Jerry Van Meter

– 3 –

The Bet

Enid Morning News, September 18, 1945
• *Oklahoma Flour Mills Face Shutdown - Wheat Shortage* •
• *Swift Reconversion Reduces Government Orders 80% to Factories* •
• *New DDT Insect Spray Hits Market, Dubbed "New Wonder of the Earth"* •

S moke poured out of the stovepipe in the ranch house roof. A wonderful aroma wafted through the screen door as Jerry approached for dinner. He loved this time of year. One of the best months in Oklahoma, September meant warm days and nights and, often, an unexpected storm that freshened and cooled the air—like the one last night. For Jerry, the small white frame house and its inviting porch conjured up lively memories of a time when his grandmother, Ida, was alive. Jerry and his four brothers would play in the giant barn, and later gather around the kitchen table for one of Grandma Ida's great meals. She had cooked on the same Majestic wood stove that Rolla still used.

Jerry arrived at six o'clock sharp; Rolla Goodnight admired promptness as much as he did cleanliness. Frank was setting the table when Jerry walked in; he looked up and smiled. Dressed in clean, pressed clothes, Frank wore his gray hair in his customary two long braids.

Rolla and Frank good-naturedly wrangled over the way to do everything, from shoeing a horse to making a pot of beans, but in their sixty-three years of friendship they both had become good cooks. Jerry knew what they had prepared even before he saw the pot roast; its aroma made his mouth water. A pitcher of iced tea sat next to several

15

bowls of food on the table, rivulets of condensation cascading down the pitcher's side, leaving a ring of moisture on the blue table cloth.

The three men spent the next few minutes swapping bowls and carrying on idle conversation. Finally they began to eat. Jerry was quietly enjoying his supper when he began to feel something strange. He looked up. Both men were staring at him. "What's going on? Did I miss something?"

Frank chuckled. "You shoulda stuck around last night."

"I made a bet with Jimmy Wakely," Rolla said. The characteristic twinkle in his eyes was gone, replaced by a serious expression. Jerry shot Frank a questioning glance and then smiled, relieved to see his familiar grin. It lit up Frank's weathered face, already made impish by his crossed left eye.

Rolla spoke up. "You know, Jerry, I don't believe in gambling. I never done anything like this in my life. But Jimmy spouted all this stuff about cities exploding and ranching going to hell. He sounded so sure about it, I got a bit riled. Besides, it's the principle. Anyway, one thing led to another and I bet him."

"Bet him what?" Jerry said and resumed eating.

"Now when I tell you, don't go gettin' in a lather. It won't be until spring. I bet Jimmy you would make a little ride. He bet you couldn't do it."

"How *little* of a ride?"

Frank, silently watching the exchange, piped up. "Movie star country, boy. Hollywood, California."

Jerry's fork paused mid-air. "Hollywood? We're half-way across the country from Hollywood."

Rolla nodded. "Jimmy said cowboyin' is dead. He says our whole way of life is all but gone. Worse yet, he says there's not a cowboy around anymore worth his salt. That didn't sit right with me."

"I still don't see what Hollywood has to do with it."

Rolla ran his finger over an imaginary line on the table cloth. "Well, it's about fifteen hundred miles to Hollywood and Jimmy lives not far from there. Frank 'n me figured the stretch of Goodnight-Loving Trail between the Brazos and Denver was about that long. It used to take us three months to take a herd that far, depending on weather and how much trouble we run into. Jimmy and I hassled back and forth and I finally said that without a bunch of cows to slow you down, you could ride to Hollywood in fifty days, maybe less."

"Yessiree, that's what he said. I heard it with my own ears." Frank was eating fast, talking between bites. Jerry sat quietly, letting the words sink in. *Grandpa made a bet based on me being tough. I'm not tough. If I were I'd be a navy pilot by now. I have no idea whether I can do that.* Jerry cleared his throat. "Fifteen hundred miles in fifty days? That's thirty miles a day, every day for almost two months." *That doesn't leave any room if something goes wrong. If I got hurt, I could mess my back up for good. The navy all over again.*

His grandfather and Frank were talking but Jerry didn't hear them. The slow fire started in his gut again when he thought about the random, rotten luck. Anger quickly surfaced, then a darker feeling even more disturbing stirred within him; it was a feeling Jerry thought he'd laid to rest. At the mention of a challenge, any challenge that put him to the test, fear galloped back into Jerry's mind like a wild mustang. *I don't want any more life-altering surprises, more hospitals and pain, or being afraid I'll never walk again.*

Apprentice Seaman Jerry Van Meter had reported to the U.S. Navy Air Corps at Warrensburg State Teachers College in Missouri one week after he graduated from Guthrie High School in Guthrie, Oklahoma. He and his squadron reported for duty, anxious to learn weather, navigation, and elementary aviation—a tough program. Jerry studied hard. Upon completion he would graduate to flight school in Pensacola and learn to fly P-40s or Curtis Interceptors for the navy. That's what he'd hoped for and dreamed about until the inter-squadron baseball game.

When the smelling salts brought him around, the doctor asked Jerry if he could wiggle his toes. Jerry tried but nothing happened. The ensign who doubled as Jerry's weather instructor and part-time coach, and big Moose Malone, the center fielder who ran into him, stood next to the doctor at the foot of the bed. All three faces were white as sheets. "Try one more time, Jerry," the doctor said. Jerry tried again. Pain swamped his entire body, radiating from the base of his skull down through his back and into every limb. Sweat broke out on his forehead as he kept trying. When his toes moved slightly, he watched panic change to relief on each face.

Jerry's dream of being a navy fighter pilot, and after the war flying for one of the airlines, had all vanished in the time it took to catch a baseball. He didn't remember the collision or being carried off on a stretcher, or the ambulance ride to the Warrensburg hospital. He did remember waking up in a fog, body aching all over, and a terrible, terrible headache. Three frightening months of pain followed, three months of wondering if he would ever walk again. His squadron buddies dropped by for an occasional visit but never stayed long. How could they visit with Jerry flat on his back, his head and neck immobilized with heavy traction.

Then came "*the Meeting.*" If he closed his eyes, Jerry could still picture the grave expression on his squadron commander's face. "The doctor wants to transfer you to the Great Lakes Naval Hospital in Chicago, Jerry. They have better facilities to deal with this sort of problem. Maybe they can help you without surgery. The three discs you ruptured are going to take special treatment. I'm sorry, son. You'll lose too much time as a result of this injury. There's no way you can catch up with the program. The navy will give you an honorable discharge, but your navy career is over." *Your navy career is over—* those five words dashed his dream. Despair grabbed the pit of his stomach. *My future shot to hell.*

Jerry took a deep breath and cleared his throat, suddenly aware that Rolla and Frank were staring at him with identical puzzled expressions. "I'll have to think about this, Grandpa," Jerry said hoarsely.

"But, Jerry, I already made the bet! I told Wakely you'd do it."

Jerry could hear the disappointment and frustration in his grandfather's voice, and see it on his face.

He jumped to his feet. "I'm sorry, Grandpa." Jerry grabbed his hat from the back of the chair and bolted for the door.

As the screen door snapped shut, Jerry heard his grandfather. "What in the world is the matter with that boy?"

Jerry saddled Buster and rode out in the prairie, heading where he always went when he wanted to be alone. Buster's steady canter took them to a thin, gouged-out streambed lined with red cedars, cottonwoods, and elms. They arrived just as the sun began its final descent toward the horizon.

Trail Creek served as Jerry's place of solace. Nestled at the convergence of two low hills, it looked out over the prairie. Lush and green in the spring, the hills were golden now, washed with the colors of the setting sun. The ever-present wind rustled the trees, scattering their leaves along the dry creek bed. Jerry sat down with his back against a bent cedar, watching as Buster began to graze. The sun's red and orange fingers reached out from the horizon, daring him to look west, taunting him for being afraid. Jerry squinted as the colors deepened. "Damn, I hate this feeling," he said to his horse. "*Boy*. Grandpa and Frank always call me *boy*. If I don't make the ride, I'll never be more than that in their minds."

Buster moved close and nudged his shoulder. "You ever been afraid, Buster? I don't think Grandpa and Frank have. How could I admit being scared to the likes of them? They have no idea how lucky I am just to be walking. After all the things they've done in their lives, there's no way they could understand. If I try this and fail, I'm not worth my salt. And if I don't try I'm a coward." Buster moved away; Jerry could tell he wanted to go back to the ranch.

It was dark by the time Jerry rode back to the Bar R. He wanted to forget the navy and the year of pain, forget wondering whether he'd ever feel good again. He wanted to be courageous and see that his grandfather and Frank were proud of him. Instead, he'd told them he had to think about it and there was no mistaking the look on their faces.

– 4 –

The Truth Comes Out

Enid Daily Eagle, September 19, 1945
• *900,000 Shares Traded In Stock Market Dip* •
• *Oklahoma Cowboy Champion To Be Named In 3 Day Event* •
• *Sammy Snead In Lead For $10,000 Prize, Southwest Invitation Golf Tourney* •

Not one to avoid confrontations, Jerry approached his grandfather first thing Wednesday morning. He found Rolla and Frank in the barn working on the Farm-All tractor, arguing about the best way to fix it. Frank already had his six guns strapped on and seemed to be winning. "Now listen here, I'm older 'n you, and I was fixin' these things when you was still in didies."

Rolla looked down at Frank who was a good six inches shorter. "You're only ten dadgum years older and I can fix this tractor in my sleep, why I—"

"Good morning, Grandpa. You too, Frank."

An instant smile appeared on Frank's face. "Top of the mornin', boy. You feelin' better?"

"Don't ask him how he's feelin' right off. Don't you know nothing?" Rolla looked at Jerry, his expression guarded. "Mornin', boy."

Rolla and Frank stood looking at Jerry expectantly. Like mismatched bookends—one short, one tall—they had been riding, ranching, and cowboying together since 1885. Cowboys through and through, Rolla and Frank's belief in Jerry landed him at this critical point where he needed to make a decision. Ever since he could remember, Jerry had run to keep up with the two of them. They were forever imprinted in his mind as a pair, and here they stood side-by-side like two halves of a circle that didn't match, imperfect but inseparable. And he loved them both.

Jerry sat down on a bale of hay and motioned for them to do the same. "It's both of you calling me *boy* that I'd like to talk about, plus I want to tell you something." Rolla and Frank sat down across from him, glancing furtively at each other and then down at their boots like elderly Huck Finns dreading a lecture. "I've never told you about the navy, about what happened. I'd like for you to hear it."

Frank leaned forward expectantly, elbows resting on his knees as he listened, nodding that he understood. His expression turned sad when Jerry told him what his commander said. Rolla leaned back against a post, chin cupped in his hand as he seemed to be weighing each word. Jerry told them about going up to catch a ball and colliding with Moose Malone, then waking up in pain and the doctors not being sure he'd walk again. He spoke about his hopes for a flying career, about his anger and bitter disappointment when the dream vanished in the blink of an eye. For the first time since it happened, Jerry revealed the doubt and anguish the accident had caused and how the prospect of this ride brought it all back. "My buddies are finishing flight school in Pensacola about now, wearing wings on their chests. I should be there with them."

"Well, I'll be," Frank said, "I never give it a thought how that changed things for you."

"I always wondered what really happened. I'm glad you finally said something," Rolla said. He started to rise.

Jerry held up his hand, a signal to wait. "I don't know how else to say this, but you two calling me *boy* makes me feel pretty useless." Their identical expressions towards each other, open mouths and raised eyebrows, made Jerry smile.

Frank spoke up first. "Do I call you that?" Jerry nodded but said nothing. "Well, I'll be dawg, must be habit. It don't mean I think of you that way. Why, you shoulda heard your grandpa 'n me tellin' Jimmy what a fine cowboy you are. We both said us old cowboys got nothin' on you. Didn't we, Rolla?"

Rolla seemed not to hear him; he squinted at Jerry. "Is that why you had to think about going on the ride? Because you got hurt and didn't get to fly? You think Frank 'n me consider you a boy because of that?"

Jerry looked down. "I said I had to think about it because I'm not sure I can make it without messing up my back. And I don't know why you call me *boy."*

"Maybe the good Lord never meant for you to fly, Jerry." Rolla's voice softened. "Sometimes bad things happen, but like riding a bronc you can't let it make you afraid. You are the best cowboy in these parts. Frank 'n me know it. The ranch hands know it. Everybody knows it. That's something to be proud of. You 'n me are Goodnights. We don't let anything stop us. Why, I never had a body work harder for me—hurt back and all—than you." Ordinarily Rolla was a man of few words except when he and Frank recounted one of their escapades or he got going on politics. He got up from the bale of hay and paced back and forth between Jerry and Frank. "If you don't like us callin' you boy, speak your mind. Just say dammitall, don't call me that." Rolla looked at Frank questioningly; Frank nodded. Rolla stopped walking and turned his intense blue eyes on Jerry. "You can do this ride, Jerry. Now that I know the whole story about the navy, I think you need to do it, to prove to yourself what Frank 'n me already know —that you can." Jerry could feel his grandfather's excitement building. "Jimmy said this country is changing fast. If he's right, this may be your only chance to do something like this. Far as I know, nobody's ever done it before. You remember me telling you how Charlie Goodnight loved adventures? Well, Frank and me had lots of 'em in our day. We look back on those as some of the best times we ever had."

"You always liked hearin' about 'em," Frank added. Jerry nodded.

"Well that's what this is, the chance of a lifetime. Your own adventure."

"But what if—"

Rolla shook his head. "If something happens along the way, you'll handle it. It'll come natural what to do and you'll do it. You can show Jimmy Wakely and the rest of them Hollywood cowboys what being a Goodnight means, what being a *real* cowboy is."

Jerry stood up and put his hands on his hips. He and Rolla eyed each other. Frank rose, looking first at one, then the other as though watching a tennis match. "Well?" Rolla said.

Jerry turned his gaze first on Frank and then on his grandfather. "Dammitall, I don't want either one of you calling me boy anymore."

Rolla nodded emphatically. "You won't hear that from me again."

"Me neither," Frank echoed.

"Thank you," Jerry said.

Rolla and Frank's expressions telegraphed the same message of understanding. Two cantankerous, charismatic, funny, hardworking men, to whom the word "cowboy" meant honor and courage. Men of integrity spawned in a wild, lawless era that slid into history on industrial-greased skids. Jerry realized the two of them could adapt only so far. Rolla, seventy-five, and Frank, eighty-five, didn't want to hear that everything they had once been and stood for would soon be forgotten, remembered only in movies. They don't deserve that, Jerry thought. He sensed it was up to him to capture time and hold onto it for them. *I must be loco. Anything can happen. I may be making the biggest mistake of my life.* Jerry glanced over at Buster still in his stall. "That horse wouldn't make it to the Texas border, let alone all the way to Hollywood." Rolla and Frank stared at him with non-comprehending looks. Then Frank broke into a grin, stepped forward and slapped Jerry on the shoulder. "I'm proud of you, b…Jerry, real proud."

Rolla smiled and offered his hand. "Me, too, son. Is it okay if I still call you that?"

Jerry shook his outstretched hand. "That's fine, Grandpa."

Frank cleared his throat. "I hate to break up this lovin' moment, but I got somethin' important to say." He had a dead-serious look on his face. "I got a horse that can make it to Hollywood and then some, that mare of mine, Fancy."

"I couldn't borrow your horse, Frank." Jerry said. "What would you ride?"

"I'll ride that buckskin we broke this spring. Besides, I'm not talkin' about you borrowin' anything. She's yours." Frank's eyes sparkled with excitement.

"Fancy is a beautiful horse. That's way too much."

"She's an Osage Indian pony, Jerry. Once I give her to you, I can't take her back. I'd run into terrible luck." Frank shook his head, his braids flopping back and forth. "No more talk about this, no sir!"

"Well then, thanks to Frank here, I got the horse," Jerry said. "So, how much money do I have to worry about you losing?" He looked at his grandfather.

Rolla slapped Frank on the back, a grin lighting up his face. "You ornery old cuss. For once you're right. Fancy's perfect for the ride." Rolla turned to Jerry. "Don't concern yourself about the money. That's between me and Mr. Hollywood. I ain't worried. The bet's important, but this is about somethin' a whole lot bigger 'n money. Jimmy thinks movie cowboys are all that's left. Hogwash! I say cowboyin' is still a good way of life, somethin' to be proud of. *That's* what this is about."

Jerry shook his head at the decision he'd just made. "Riding a horse to Hollywood, even one as good as Fancy, is damned sure getting there the hard way. But the two of you are right. I've been training for this my whole life, without even realizing it. You and Frank taught me everything I need to get me there."

The three headed for the ranch house for breakfast, Jerry walking in the middle. He could feel Frank's excitement; his step was even livelier than usual and he couldn't stop talking. "Now we got the winter to brush up on his cowboyin'," Frank said as they neared the house. "Think that's enough time, Rolla?"

"It will be if you let *me* do it," Rolla said in a droll voice.

"Listen here, I was cowboyin' when you was in didies. There ain't no way I'm gonna let you be in charge."

My God, what have I gotten myself into?

– 5 –

Travel Light, a Race Against Time

United Press Service, December 1945

• *Synthetic Oil Developed, Two City Try-Out In East Planned* •
• *Automotive Engineers Predict 1947 Production of
Rear Engine Passenger Car* •
• *Plastic Foam, Secret War Material, Hits Commercial Market* •

Jerry's ride, his route, and what he should take with him dominated Rolla and Frank's conversations during the entire winter, discussions that turned lively at times and were usually followed by laughter. Frank rarely rode back to his Perkins home, fearful that Rolla would "mess up Jerry's training." Their planning sessions invariably turned into "do you remember that time we…" so Jerry let them talk. He pored over maps, trying to anticipate problems, making notes about the terrain, and logging distances between campsites and supply stops.

The Oklahoma prairie contained large ranches, but for the most part remained open rangeland dissected by country dirt roads. Jerry assumed the Texas Panhandle would be the same. He planned to ride southwest until he intersected Route 66 then follow it all the way to Amarillo where he would stock up on supplies. After visiting Charlie Goodnight's Palo Duro Canyon, he would drop farther south and travel over the *Llano Estacado*—the high plains of New Mexico—to the base of the Rockies. Riding cross-country, Jerry planned to hunt and fish along the way. He charted his route to pass through a town at least every four days when his supplies would need replenishing. *Travel light, a race against time.*

Jerry's training with Rolla and Frank proved to be good medicine for helping him forget flying, his back injury, and the navy. Frank practiced the fast-draw with him several hours every day with empty Colt .45s until Jerry could draw lightning fast. And when they finished, his grandfather tossed tin cans into the air and had Jerry fire at them with his Winchester until he did not miss. "Sometimes you only get one shot at a rabbit or quail. I don't want you to go hungry," Rolla said.

Working with five-year-old Fancy proved to be even better medicine for Jerry. A pinto, Fancy stood sixteen hands high with sturdy white legs and a white blaze. She had a slick coat, broad red-brown breast and neck, with pure white flanks and wide, brown hindquarters. Fancy followed Jerry around like an eleven-hundred-pound puppy, responding to voice commands quicker than any horse he'd ever trained. She craved attention and nudged Jerry if he ignored her. With her wide-set eyes, brown forelock and white and brown mane that followed exactly the break in her coloring, Fancy was indeed a beautiful horse—and tireless. She astounded Jerry with her stamina and speed.

But the name Fancy didn't suit her; it sounded prissy. She loved water. She liked to roll in dirt or mud; it didn't matter. Ornery when she wanted to be, playful, always hungry, she was anything but fancy. Jerry had timed her. She could "fan right on down the road"—that is she had a running walk of eight miles an hour, faster than any horse he'd ever seen. He asked Frank if he could shorten her name to Fan.

"She belongs to you now. You can call her Matilda if you want," Frank said. "She'll get you there, but I'm tellin' you that horse'll eat a swath of grass from here to California wide enough to see from one of them aeroplanes."

Jerry laughed and patted the mare's flank. "Okay, Fan. Eat your way to California, but we just have to make sure we get there in fifty days—together."

Jerry took a week off at Christmas and went home to Guthrie, his first holiday with his parents since he'd left for Missouri. Both parents worked at Tinker Air Field in Oklahoma City, but Edna Van Meter always made Christmas special. She and Vearl and the boys had decorated a tree. Everyone had gifts, and she cooked a huge dinner of turkey, dressing and gravy, and three kinds of pie that filled the house with delicious smells. "Grandpa and Frank are good cooks, so don't tell them I said this, but this is the best meal I've had in a year," Jerry told her.

The whole family was there except for his eldest brother, Jimmy, still in the navy flying transports between California and Guam. The other boys clamored for Jerry's attention. Bill, who was twelve, showed him newspaper clippings about his hero, Bob Feller returning from a four-year hitch in the navy to pitch again for the Cleveland Indians. Sixteen-year-old David laid out possum and skunk hides he'd prepared for sale and then he and Jerry pored over the latest comic books that David had gotten from the Guthrie Owl Drug. Byron, eleven, made Jerry practice fast-draws with him and then begged to go on the ride to California. Jerry's father refused to discuss the trip.

Vearl Van Meter was handsome and athletic, but a serious man. A talented baseball player who had made it as far as the minor leagues, he never got any farther. An impending war, a wife, five sons, and an eighty-acre farm precluded any career in professional baseball. The boys helped him tend the family's four milk cows, their work horses and mules, and care for a large flock of chickens that provided a steady income from local stores. Vearl taught them to hunt and fish, to play baseball, and other practical things boys should know, like how to fix things around the farm. But what he wanted most was for his sons to go to college and excel in sports. Suffering from ulcers, Vearl spent his spare time reading. He never shared in Jerry and Byron's love of horses, but Edna Goodnight Van Meter did; she was an accomplished rider.

Edna also inherited her father Rolla's happy nature and his blond, blue-eyed good looks. Slender and strong, Edna could ride, can vegetables and fruits, cook, and out-run all her kids at tag or hide and seek. She admired Norman Rockwell's art and loved nothing better than gathering Vearl and the boys around the kitchen table at night for pie and listening to "Fibber McGee and Molly" or "Gene Autry's Melody Ranch" on the radio.

In a rare moment alone at that table before returning to the Bar R, Jerry talked to his mother about the ride. She sat peeling apples into a bowl, glancing at her son. "You seem uncertain, Jerry. So why are you doing it?"

"You know how Grandpa and Frank are. This is really important to them. They're as excited as a couple of kids. You think I'm making a mistake?"

"I know your grandfather and Frank only too well. What I think is, don't do it unless it's *your* dream. Not for anyone but yourself."

"How about it, Mom, you think I can make it?"

Edna smiled. "You've wanted to be a cowboy, like Dad and Frank, since you could walk. One minute you were riding a stick horse, and the next thing I knew they had you handling a real one fifteen hands high, and you six years old." His mother got up and washed her hands and came back with two coffees. "After they'd taught you to ride and rope, hunt and track—all the things they loved—you upped and decided you wanted to be a pilot. You and Jimmy then built those models and flew them, both of you talking nothing but airplanes. Dad and Frank were crushed. If you're only doing it for them, don't. They'll get over it."

"You didn't answer my question. Do you believe I can make it?"

Edna covered his hand with hers. "Remember when you wanted to be Buck Rogers and fly to the moon? I might have to think on that. Not this. I know you can make it, son, but you're the one who has to believe, not me."

Jerry rode Fan the fifty miles back to the Bar R in a norther'. Blown by a wind straight out of the north, freezing rain came at them horizontally in sheets. Jerry lowered his hat and pulled his rain slicker tighter. "A little test," he said to Fan. She acted like she was out for a Sunday romp, oblivious to the conditions.

They got back to the Bar R at dusk. Jerry dried Fan off and brushed her. "This was one day, not fifty, but as bad as it was, we made it in a little under six hours." He put Fan's blanket on and gave her rolled oats and hay. "You're making this trip seem a lot more possible, girl."

During the next months Jerry used one of the ranch quarter horses for his work, but as soon as he finished each day he trained with Fan. Searching out rock-strewn trails on the Bar R's varied terrain, Jerry and Fan rode up and down hills and through its canyons. Fan pranced; she rolled in the mud, and she ate. They went out in storms, into swollen rivers, and rode at all hours of the day or night. Fan wasn't afraid of deep water or fast currents. And each day when he took care of her, Jerry poured out his hopes and misgivings, his restless feelings. Fan yawned; she slept; she looked at Jerry with attentive eyes, swishing her tail, flicking her ears back and forth. He accepted her behavior as nonverbal assent.

Jerry celebrated his twentieth birthday on February 13, 1946. He now wore the special belt on his back only when he did heavy work. Unaware of the subtle shift taking place in his feelings about the ride, visions of adventure replaced fear. He imagined living on the trail like Frank and Rolla, like Jesse Chisholm and Charlie Goodnight and the cowboys before them. In his daydreams, Jerry conquered every obstacle; he envisioned riding triumphantly along palm-lined boulevards into warm sunny Hollywood. They trained until Jerry completed his spring work. At that point it seemed pointless to train any more. The horse never faltered; she performed like a champion.

The last day of April 1946, Fan had drunk her fill of water and stood swishing her tail, patiently waiting while he finished brushing her. She looked at Jerry, her expression and demeanor indicating she wanted her hay and oats.

"So, you want dinner, do you? Have I trained you or is it the other way around?" He stroked her withers as she devoured her hay. "Dammitall, Fan, we can do this ride."

The pinto stared at him as she chomped through her hay.

"It started out as Grandpa's dream, but I can feel it, Fan. You were born to make this ride. So was I."

– 6 –

Final Preparations

The Clinton Daily News, May 2, 1946
• *Standard Oil Survey Declares Jet Planes Impractical for Peacetime Aviation* •
• *Missouri Sheriff Sues Oklahoma Sheriff Over 600 Fifths of Confiscated Liquor* •

Jerry's spent Thursday, May 2nd, his last day at the Bar R, getting his supplies ready for the trip. He gathered up a bedroll, a rain slicker, a one-gallon canteen of water, maps, compass, a pair of Finch pliers, a frying pan, and coffee pot. The saddlebags held enough food staples for a few days, including a pint jar of sourdough biscuit starter that Rolla and Frank reminded him ten times not to forget. Finally he loaded twenty pounds of grain for Fan, a box of salt, two extra horse shoes and a blanket for Fan.

The ranch hands slapped Jerry on the back and laughingly warned him, "Be careful of them Hollywood starlets. If you see Lana Turner or Rita Hayworth, get us a pin-up picture, will ya?" Jerry promised he would.

His grandfather motioned Jerry to follow him into the house. Rolla went into his bedroom and returned with an unwrapped box. "You'll be needing these," he said.

"I can't believe this, Grandpa." Jerry lifted a pair of hand-tooled silver spurs, one of his grandfather's prized possessions, out of the box. "These are the spurs Elmer Spark made especially for you." The box also held one hundred fifty dollars, the equivalent of a month's pay, and twenty silver dollars.

Rolla nodded. "I want you to have the spurs. Call your Mama once in a while and let us know you're all right, hear?" Jerry stood staring at the spurs. He heard the screen door bang shut; his grandfather had exited. Taking a last look around the kitchen, Jerry tried to stamp its familiar sights and smells into his memory—at the moment coffee and bacon with a little floor wax thrown in; the old linoleum glistened in the morning sun. Smiling at his grandfather's penchant for neatness and order, Jerry clipped the spurs on his boots.

Frank and Rolla were standing near Fan when Jerry came out, his spurs jingling with each step. Frank let out a whistle as Jerry stepped down off the porch. "Ain't you purty."

The ranch hands whistled and clapped as Jerry shoved the Winchester .22 in the scabbard hanging from his saddle. He said goodbye to each man with a handshake, then they politely disappeared. Jerry held out his hand to his grandfather. "Thank you for the spurs and the chance to do this. You believed in me even when I didn't. I want to win that bet more than anything."

"You'll do it. You just had to put some things behind you," Rolla said. "I'm hoping the world out there ain't changin' as fast as Jimmy said, but I expect you'll let us know." He let go of Jerry's hand and ambled off toward the barns. When it came to saying goodbye to his grandfather, Jerry knew it would be brief.

Frank stood by watching the others. When Rolla walked away he stepped forward. "I never seen California. Wish I was goin' with you."

"I know, I do, too, Frank. I'll send some pictures soon as I get there."

"One of the ocean'd be nice."

"Look for it in the mail about the end of June."

Frank shook Jerry's hand and stared up at him, a wistful expression on his face. It seemed he had something else to say, but remained silent. Jerry spoke up. "Don't worry about me, Frank. I remember everything you taught me. My back's doing better and Fan is the best horse in Oklahoma."

"Guess that's about it then. Except this." Frank removed one of the Colt .45s from his holster and handed it to Jerry. "I been usin' this six-shooter since Judge Parker over at Fort Smith made me a deputy marshal. Them varmints that killed my father saw the smokin' end of this gun—last thing they ever did see. It shoots straight and true and I want you to have it. It's a lot better 'n that thing you're packin'."

Jerry started to protest; Frank interrupted. "And I'm gonna tell you what old Mose Beaman told me: never aim your gun at anythin' but what you want to kill, and—"

"I know." Jerry grinned. "Fill your hand, you sonofabitch," they said in unison.

Frank chuckled. "Well, I'll be dawg, you have been listening."

"I don't know what to say, Frank." Frank was never without both of his six-shooters. One of his favorite sayings, "I'd rather have a pocket full of rocks than a empty gun," he'd heard a hundred times. Frank had carried this Colt since he was seventeen years old. It had six notches in it. He held out his hand for Jerry's gun. Jerry handed it to him and holstered the Colt. "Thanks seems pretty slim, but I'm going to say it anyway. Thank you for everything, Frank. For Fan, for the gun, for teaching me. Don't worry. None of it went to waste. And I'll be able to tell some tales of my own when I get back."

Frank chuckled. "It's about time we got some new stories." He turned and walked toward the barns. Jerry swung into the saddle, turned Fan around, and set her out at a trot. When they reached the gate of the Bar R, he looked back over his shoulder. Rolla, hands on his hips, stood silhouetted against the light of the open barn door, Frank at his side. Frank had pushed his giant cowboy hat back on his forehead. They waved. Jerry touched the brim of his Stetson and headed Fan south toward Guthrie. He would spend tomorrow with his mom, dad, and brothers and leave for California early the following day.

Jerry arrived in Guthrie at five in the afternoon and found Vearl, Edna, and Byron talking to someone. A man with a camera in his hand stood leaning against a dusty black Ford. Byron came running up to Jerry, his eyes wide with excitement. "Jerry, guess what?" He pointed at the man. "He's a reporter from *The Guthrie Daily Leader*!"

"Why's he here?" Jerry asked as he rode up.

"He heard about your ride. You're gonna be in the newspaper!" Byron shouted. Jerry brought Fan to a halt a few feet away from the group.

"I'd like to get a picture," the reporter said as he aimed his camera. "So, you're riding Fancy all the way to Hollywood on a bet, are you?"

Jerry smiled at the comment just as the reporter snapped the picture. "Her name is Fan and that's exactly what I'm going to do."

Jerry Van Meter on Fan, May 2, 1946.
Photo courtesy of Guthrie Daily Leader and Jerry Van Meter

– 7 –

Call Collect Anytime

The Guthrie Daily Leader, May 4, 1946
• *Jerry Van Meter and Fan Have Eye on Hollywood* •
• *Ben McGriff, Guthrie Negro, Found Guilty of Manslaughter* •
• *General Bradley's Plane Delivers Iron Lung to Muskogee for Texas Veteran* •

Jerry made the most of his short visit in Guthrie. He rechecked his supplies, spent time with each of his three brothers, and went over his route with his mother and father. Vearl relented and took part in the discussion this time. Jerry hardly slept that night. Saturday morning arrived with the sun hiding behind low clouds; he stepped outside. A heavy mist hung over the garden and trees as Jerry headed toward the old log barn. Inside, dressed and trail-ready Byron greeted him, "I'm going." His pony stood saddled, a bedroll and knapsack slung over his rump.

"We talked about this, remember? Mom said you couldn't go. You've got school to finish, Byron. Besides, this might end up being a rough trip."

"Puleese, Jerry, I'll be good. I won't be any trouble. I got plenty of peanut butter and jelly." Byron's chin stuck out at a defiant angle though his eyes were holding back tears.

"I wish you could go, cowboy, but you can't. Let's ask Mom to let you ride a little way with me. We can pretend, okay?" They led their horses out into the yard. Edna emerged out the back door, an apron over her wash dress.

"And where do you think you are going, Byron Van Meter?"

At her tone, Byron released his unshed tears. "I want to go with Jerry. Why can't—"

Jerry put his hand on Byron's shoulder. "Would it be okay if Byron rode as far as the Eggleston place? It'll give us a chance to talk and I'll make him promise to ride straight back."

Edna came forward and kissed Jerry on the cheek. "Please be careful, son. Call collect anytime and write for sure, hear?" She put her hand under Byron's chin and tilted his face upward. "All right, young man, but I'm trusting you to keep your word. Not another inch farther than the Eggleston place then you turn around and come right home. Promise?"

Byron hung his head. "Promise," he said softly.

David and Bill came out of the house, pulling on their shirts, followed by a worried-looking Vearl. They exchanged quick good-byes, then Jerry and Byron mounted their horses and galloped away, waving their hats like the movie cowboys they loved.

"Yahoo," Byron hollered as soon as they were out of earshot.

His little brother rode three miles with Jerry, all the while pretending they were running from outlaws. He kept up a stream of pretend chatter, and then became quiet as they reached the edge of their neighbor's ranch.

"Okay, Byron, this is as far as you go. I want you to ride straight home. I'll send a card on the trip, a special one just for you. Okay?" Jerry and Byron hugged awkwardly atop their horses and then Jerry turned Fan and trotted off. A short distance away he looked back. Byron was staring after him, tears streaming down his face. Jerry reined Fan to a halt, turned her around and waved his hat like they always did. He waited. Byron stood up in his stirrups and waved back, his goodbye lost in the distance and his tears. "Bye, cowboy," Jerry called out. He turned Fan and whacked her on the rump with his hat. He dared not look back. Jerry rode hard until he and Fan were well away from the Eggleston Ranch.

When the early fog dissipated, the dazzling prairie sun hung high in the sky. West and south of Guthrie, lush green wheat fields covered the landscape broken only by stands of cottonwood, jack pine, and elm. A breeze rolled across the top of the wheat, creating rippling waves of light and dark green. Jerry passed red dirt roads that crooked their way through fields toward clapboard houses where irises bloomed in profusion. Rusty farm equipment sat not far from clothes lines with overalls, work shirts, and bed sheets blowing stiff in the wind.

Jerry crossed the Snake, the Cox, and the Pawnee, creeks that ran full, each one lined by a dense thicket of trees. Fat, shiny horses grazed in huge pastures dotted with Herefords and lanky Longhorns. He encountered an occasional fence, usually barbed wire stapled to wooden posts. Jerry used his Finch pliers to pull the staples out from three or four posts, offering slack for Fan to safely pass and then tacked the wire back in place. In the distance, grain silos rose from the horizon like rural skyscrapers.

"Do you feel like we're on vacation, Fan?" She wanted to run but Jerry held her to a jog and lope gait, trying to pace the frisky mare. He had to average a minimum of thirty miles every day to win the bet. *Whatever the bet is.*

He'd never known his grandfather to gamble. And from the stories Jerry had heard, Charlie Goodnight adamantly opposed gambling, even forbidding his trail hands to play poker. He once fired three of his four wranglers on a cattle drive because he'd caught them gambling after he had warned them twice. Charlie's action left only himself and one other man to drive two thousand head of cattle. Principle mattered to Charlie Goodnight.

Jerry was three years old in 1929 when Charlie Goodnight passed away. Though they never met, he felt a kinship with the man. Rolla and Frank had told him stories about Charlie for as far back as he could remember. Rolla admired him, called him Uncle Charlie as a term of respect, though they were "cousins a couple of times removed," Rolla said. Both men were self-educated, tireless, charismatic, and independent. They epitomized the pioneer spirit and were protective of their way of life. That Rolla had bet Jimmy Wakely in the first place, and a bet that would take Jerry from his chores at the Bar R for several months in the second place, did not fit his grandfather's character. But he *had* made the bet. That spoke volumes to Jerry about the importance of this ride.

Three days out, Jerry and Fan reached Clinton, Oklahoma and made their nightly camp near Route 66. They crossed the highway—empty at the moment—and paused at its edge to look east and west. It stretched across the flat landscape into infinity, a ribbon of promise that had transported countless Okies west in their flivers, Model Ts, and every other means of transportation. Piled high with kids and possessions, sometimes with chickens and farm animals thrown in, Okies had run from blinding dust and grinding poverty to California. As long as Jerry could remember, everyone called California, "the land of milk and honey." Now it was his destination.

Jerry and Fan arrived at the Mother Road at supper time. He made camp on the south side, away from the highway. Cars went by, silent from his distance, their headlights arcing flashes of color in the disappearing light. A steady stream of big trucks thundered past. The breeze lofted the whine of their cranked-up diesel engines over his camp then just as quick disappeared, the sound gobbled up by the forever-landscape. In the intervals between the cars and trucks, Jerry heard the familiar sounds of crickets, chattering ground squirrels, and later the yip-yip-yip of coyotes in the distance.

Jerry's pot beans tasted bland compared to the beans Frank and Rolla made, and his sourdough biscuits got slightly burned on the bottom. But he washed everything down with strong coffee and promised himself that his cooking would get better. After supper, Jerry sat by his campfire watching the lights race past, picturing movie stars, palm-lined boulevards, and miles of sandy beaches as he wondered what adventures awaited him.

– 8 –

A Mean Place

The Amarillo Globe News, May 8, 1946
• *Truman Wants Traffic Rules Tightened, to Prevent "Nuts & Morons"*
From Buying Licenses •
• *Amarillo Man's Essay Wins Him a Flying Fortress B-17* •
• *Showers, Thunderstorms, Frost Due* •

On day five of their journey, Jerry and Fan left Oklahoma at Texola and rode into the Texas Panhandle. The difference was at once magnificent and terrifying. Gone were the gently rolling hills and color green of his home state; gone was any gentleness at all. The Panhandle opened into vastness that dwarfed anything he could have envisioned. Up close it appeared unforgiving and threatening, the terrain scarred only by a rare wash or draw. Stretched out before him, the sight sent a thrill through Jerry—the land's majesty and the sheer endlessness of it. Not fettered by normal life-giving growth, the landscape sprouted occasional scrub brush, mesquite, cacti, and a few scrawny cottonwoods. More noticeable were the greasewood trees whose acrid odor repelled animal and man alike. Jerry held tight to Fan's reins as thunder-heads boomed above them. He kept his eye on the rain-filled clouds scutting across the sky, the clouds driven by a fierce wind that he soon discovered was the defining characteristic of this land of extremes. Using his Finch pliers, Jerry undid the occasional barbed wire fence they encountered. After Fan crossed, he tacked it back like he found it.

For the next two days he and Fan could not escape the blowing sand. Swept from the earth as if Mother Nature were sweeping her floor, the wind flung it at them, stinging Jerry's eyes, scouring his face and hands, anything exposed. He put his red kerchief up over his nose and mouth, but even with it he could feel the dirt invade his lungs. Sand coated the both of them from head to foot, collecting around Fan's nostrils and forelock, and forming muddy rivulets in the creases of Jerry's clothes. He remembered seeing pictures of the dust storm of the thirties, of dead horses and cows lying in the dirt, choked by lack of water and overcome by dust when Oklahoma's topsoil blew out of the state on hurricane-force winds.

Jerry found a campsite at the bottom of a shallow draw where, if he hunkered down the dirt blew over his head; he felt lucky to find any respite from the conditions. Lean cottonwoods lined the shallow ditch, their twisted exposed roots snaking down into the streambed in search of moisture. The trees' wind-scarred trunks and branches, with their tenacious leaves, formed a meager shield from the wind's effects. Nevertheless, Jerry said silent thanks for the reprieve they offered from the wind as he tethered Fan to a tree. He washed her face and around her eyes with water from his canteen and covered her with her blanket. Jerry fed Fan first, stroking her neck and offering words of encouragement. She ate with her rump turned towards the wind, ears laid back in a picture of misery and irritation.

Jerry had to deal with his own brand of suffering unrelated to the hostile elements. On their second day in the Texas Panhandle, a vast, all-encompassing silence enveloped him, the feeling akin to encountering an unrelenting formidable enemy. The land's boundless space and open country, its silence so intense it made him catch his breath, was something Jerry had not counted on or given a thought to when planning the trip. They had been gone seven days; this was their third night in Texas. Each new day brought incredible vistas, excitement, and wonder. But as the day unfolded hour by hour, the quiet chased him like a predator following its prey. Jerry felt a yawning solitude, an awareness of just how small and alone he was in the vastness that surrounded him. The wind-driven rain arrived, turning the layer of dirt on Jerry's clothes to mud. Though it added to their discomfort, Jerry welcomed the rain. He spread his bedroll on the west side of the bank and unrolled one of his chaps to cover his face. Wind and rainstorm aside, he slept as soon as he closed his eyes.

Bright sunshine greeted him the next morning and, along with it, the wind. Overnight it had abated only slightly. Frozen puddles in the shady bottom of the draw were the only evidence of the night's rain. Freshness in the air was all that was left behind from what rain had fallen over the desert-plain.

Contrary to her usual demeanor, Fan was still disconsolate when he watered and fed her. Her personality had emerged with each passing day. She loved to be scratched under the chin and always stretched her neck for more. She loved apples but would also eat cookies if they were offered; she preferred rolled oats over bran—ground oats and wheat—and she liked timothy hay better than the grass or alfalfa variety.

But this morning in the middle of the Texas Panhandle, Fan had no intention of wearing a saddle. She flattened her ears and bared her big yellow teeth, backed up, sidestepped, and did everything she could to keep the saddle off. Using the trees to restrict her movement, Jerry held her reins taut with his left hand and hoisted the saddle up and onto her back with his right—a difficult maneuver even for a strong cowhand. Despite the morning's cold, sweat popped out on his forehead from the effort. "Dammitall, Fan, what's the matter with you? We gotta do this together."

Once he had secured the saddle, she seemed resigned and stood quietly watching him expectantly. Jerry bent over to retrieve his bedroll and chaps just as a gust of wind whipped over them. Off came his Stetson; the wind sent it tumbling along the ground. Before he could run after it, Fan trotted over and secured it with her teeth. Jerry stood open-mouthed and watched her walk back, then stop in front of him, his hat hanging from her mouth. Jerry's chuckle turned into a belly laugh that shook him until tears ran down his face. Like a big overgrown pup covered with dirt, Fan stood looking at him with innocent brown eyes, offering up not a stick or a ball, but one slightly slobbered-on Stetson. Jerry took his hat from her, wiped it off and placed it on his head.

"Nobody is *ever* gonna believe this, most of all Frank and Grandpa. I can't believe it myself," he said aloud, wiping his eyes with the back of his hand. "If you're trying to make up for being stubborn, you picked a damned memorable way to do it." Jerry was still smiling as they headed off, the silence temporarily forgotten. Despite the miserable conditions, they were ahead of schedule. Eight days out and they had covered two hundred fifty-five miles.

Jerry stopped for supplies at a store on 6th Street in the San Jacinto area of Amarillo, just off Route 66. Amarillo looked like a booming town. Shiny cars whizzed by them then headed off down streets lined with stately cedars, green lawns, and big brick homes. Well-dressed men and women walked along the sidewalks, their children hopscotching ahead of them. The parents smiled; the children stopped their game and waved as Jerry and Fan rode past.

He felt embarrassed by his appearance. Trail dirt covered his clothes and, though he had shaved and washed his face, he could only hope it was dirt-free. His shaving mirror fit into the palm of his hand and reflected only tiny round fragments of his face. Jerry opened the door of San Jacinto Mercantile to find the prettiest girl he'd ever seen.

Other customers gave Jerry a quick curious glance, but the pretty girl didn't seem put off by his dirt-covered clothes. When he answered "Hollywood" to her question of where he was headed, she flirted openly, asking if he was going there to be a movie star.

"Not even close." He smiled.

She introduced herself, "Claire Elizabeth Dupree," announcing her name in a soft, smooth voice, drawing out "*Dupreeee*" in a sweet Texas drawl that raised the hair on the back of Jerry's neck. Slender and petite with creamy white skin and bright red lipstick, Claire

Elizabeth wore her corn-silk blond hair rolled into a perfect pompadour. But most memorable, pretty Claire Elizabeth Dupree, who said her daddy owned the store, smelled of lavender perfume that filled the air and made Jerry take a deep breath. She rang up his groceries slowly, turning each can deliberately to find a price, weighing the individual pieces of fruit, and wrapping each egg separately in butcher paper. Claire kept up a steady stream of conversation as she asked about his trip, listening attentively to his every word. Jerry nodded and answered and watched, enthralled by her interest, mesmerized by her voice and graceful hands. A loud *whap* yanked him out of his trance; the wind had slammed a metal sign over on its side in front of the store. A customer raced past the window, chasing after his hat that the wind had stolen.

"My gosh, look at that," Jerry said. Fan jumped at the noise. Tethered securely, she pranced her hindquarters from side to side. "I've got to get my horse out of that wind." He retrieved his wallet from a back pocket. "I better hurry before she kicks somebody."

"It can get a lot worse. When it really gets ripping, we've had big trucks blow right over on their side," Claire Elizabeth said. "Sometimes it quiets down after dark, then again it might howl all night long."

"Thanks, I'll remember that." Jerry paid ninety-five cents for his purchases.

Claire Elizabeth offered her hand. "Good luck, Mr. Oklahoma cowboy. Y'all come back when you can stay longer."

Jerry reluctantly said goodbye, jammed his hat down tight, and stepped outside. He deposited his groceries into the saddle bags and threw the gunny sack with twenty pounds of rolled oats across Fan's rump. As he headed Fan across the highway, his head was still swirling with the fragrance and image of the pretty girl. Jerry directed Fan south for a short distance along the edge of a highway until they reached the outskirts of Amarillo, then turned southeastward. The minute they returned to the open plains, all images of Claire Elizabeth evaporated, scoured from Jerry's mind by the elements. The afternoon sun's glare bounced off the light-colored sand and into his eyes; the wind slammed him with dirt-laden gusts. He pulled the red kerchief up over his nose once again and pressed on. *Damn, Claire Elizabeth Dupree, why do you have to be from such a mean place?*

The difference between Jerry's Oklahoma and this part of Texas was more than the landscapes' lack of gentility. Except for Amarillo, the towns Jerry had passed were tiny, and the few people he'd seen scurried from one building to another to get out of the wind. Between towns he came across nothing but the wind-swept Panhandle, the only sign of life an occasional windmill. The troughs at these windmills provided a source of water for Fan.

In contrast, Oklahoma's prairie was covered with wheat, sorghum, and broomcorn, some of it planted the new way; not in straight rows but following the contour of the hills to prevent erosion. The visual effect was a gentle sort of beauty. West and south of Guthrie, Jerry had seen big Caterpillar graders scooping out low spots, creating farm ponds on prairie ranches. Radio newscasts claimed there would eventually be two hundred thousand farm ponds all over the state. "The water supply has to be made predictable," Governor Robert Kerr, Oklahoma's first native-born governor, had said in a radio broadcast. He also wanted lakes and reservoirs built to assure that Oklahoma would never suffer another "Dustbowl."

Jerry headed Fan southeast across weed-covered sand dunes studded with yucca and prickly pear. The wind held steady. He put his hand to his ear to lessen its noise. Total silence except Fan's breathing. He looked around—no fences, no people, only an alert-looking prairie dog peeking at them from his hole. There was nothing but sand and endless plains. He reached up to secure his Stetson and caught a whiff of Claire Elizabeth's lavender perfume on his hand. The gnawing loneliness Jerry fought to hold at bay until he could conquer it, swamped him unexpectedly out of nowhere, grabbing him in a vise that took his breath away.

Jerry shook himself and looked around, and shook himself again. He tried whistling, but couldn't with his mouth covered by his kerchief. He hummed instead and silently repeated Rolla's words: *whatever happens, you'll handle it.* After two hours of riding, Jerry at last saw the welcome signs of man as they reached the northern rim of the Palo Duro Canyon. In the distance he spotted the silhouette of several buildings; it looked like a school or college campus.

The north end of the canyon was no more than a few hundred yards wide and the same in depth. The jagged, ledge-covered walls were naturally hewn of the sun's colors, becoming richer and the layers more vivid as the last of the sun's rays settled on them. The Palo Duro was another of Mother Nature's wondrous creations, a huge fissure in the earth that disappeared into the distance a hundred miles away. Jerry wanted to ride into it, to see and smell it for himself. This canyon had once been home to a man who, though he had never met Charlie Goodnight, had shaped what Jerry believed in, and influenced the very way he lived his life.

Jerry found an old trail and it took an hour for them to descend to the floor of the former J.A. Ranch. He could only stare. Connections clicked and stories stored deep in Jerry's memory surfaced, bringing with them an acute sense of familiarity. Frank's and Rolla's words echoed in his head. "The canyon had wall-to-wall cattle, Jerry. It was a cattleman's paradise, boy. The Palo Duro ain't nothin' like you ever seen." And they were dead on. The Palo Duro was a different world from the wind-swept, barren plain above.

Between the cream, red, brown, and rust-striated sandstone walls stretched a grass range dotted with brittle red cedars, wild chinas, cottonwoods, and hackberry trees. Prairie Dog Creek ran full with tiny streams jutting off it from every direction. Leading Fan, Jerry followed the tributary to the far wall, where at the cap-rock high above the jagged ledges, the water flowed down from a spring. He walked the width of the canyon, stopping to scoop up loose dirt, briefly smell it and then watch it flow through his fingers. Kneeling beside a stream,

he washed his hands in the cold water while Fan drank. The formations, the trees, the smell of the grass all seemed familiar. Being here
was like opening the pages of one of his brother David's comic books
and stepping into an enchanted land.

Jerry first picketed Fan and then built a fire. Next he led her into
the icy waterfall where he washed off the sweat and sand from both of
them. Anxious to get rid of the caked-on mud, he laundered his clothes
and Fan's blanket and hung them on the bare branches of a red cedar
by the fire. Next, he cut a supple branch from a cottonwood and rigged
a fishing pole by attaching some string to it and a hook he'd brought
on the trip.

Soon, the aroma of pan-fried trout mingled with mesquite smoke
and sweet grass. Jerry whistled while he cooked. Picketed on a
hundred-foot rope, Fan was busy happily munching grass along the
length of it. He silently thanked his grandfather for making the bet, for
giving him this chance to experience an important part of Charlie
Goodnight's world.

The Palo Duro had been the ancestral camping grounds of the
Comanche's. Its walls, holder of centuries of secrets, formed majestic
stone formations that were more dramatic than any man could have
devised. Long after the light faded, Jerry sat staring up at more stars
than he'd ever seen before. Stories, anecdotes, and exploits paraded
before him, tales about Charlie and this famous ranch that Jerry had
heard since he was old enough to remember.

Charles Goodnight discovered the Palo Duro in 1876. Already
famous as a cattle raiser and trail driver, he claimed it, put a herd on it,
and then attracted capital from a rich Irishman, John Adair, and his
wife. Mrs. Adair happened to be the daughter of a wealthy New York
banker and the sister of a Senator. With their money, Charlie bought
more cattle—fine breeding bulls and productive cows—and coined the
JA brand in honor of the Adairs' half-million dollar investment. Over
the next few years as many as a hundred thousand head of cattle
grazed these lands and, during any one year, Charlie would easily sell

thirty thousand head. At the age of twenty—exactly Jerry's age—Charlie started his first cattle business. At age thirty he and Oliver Loving blazed the Goodnight-Loving trail which, over years of cattle drives, Loving and Goodnight continually altered but ended in the same destination, Cheyenne, Wyoming.

And it was to the Palo Duro that fifteen-year-old Rolla Goodnight rode from his home in Kansas to learn from Charlie Goodnight how to be a cowboy.

Rolla and Frank told Jerry about returning to the JA from a cattle drive to Kansas in 1884 with Charlie. On their return they discovered that Comanche Chief Quanah Parker had arrived while they were away and had brought a band of warriors, women, and children with him. When Charlie found out they were camped at the Palo Duro, he did what he always did—made a gift of a few head of cattle to Chief Parker. Frank and Rolla helped Charlie drive them to the Comanche camp. Charlie returned to the ranch house, but the two young cowboys stayed behind and spied on the celebration that followed.

After the Indians killed one of the steers and put it on a spit over the fire, they danced and drummed. Rolla and Frank told Jerry that, sixty years later, they could still hear the throbbing drums and see the warriors dancing by the fire. Jerry closed his eyes and listened. The drumbeat was silent. *Maybe they sat right here, around a fire just like this.*

Loneliness did not come this night and the silence went unnoticed. Jerry felt a sense of purpose, of well-being. He was part of this place and its history; he was destined to be here. And Charles Goodnight was here, as surely as Jerry, sharing the warmth of his fire.

The next morning, even Fan seemed in a good mood. She had eaten a good part of the circle during the night. "Frank was right about you. Wonder if they can see that from an airplane?" Jerry teased.

They rode farther into the canyon, exploring eastward until they discovered where it changed to a wider expanse. It was an endless natural range enclosed by its own sandstone bluffs; the JA Ranch was a cattle rancher's dream. And like the cattle baron who once owned it, the Palo Duro was an anomaly—heaven compared to the hostile plains above. It felt like home and Jerry hated to leave.

After a steep climb, they reached the western rim at noon. Jerry dismounted and glanced over his map and notes while Fan cooled down. He took a last look eastward as the straight-up sun sent shafts of light down into the depths. "You're part of the reason I'm here, Charlie, this Goodnight tradition and proving I'm part of it," he said quietly.

Only the wind answered him. Jerry turned Fan away from the Palo Duro and headed toward New Mexico.

Charles Goodnight and buffalo head, circa 1888.
Courtesy of Panhandle-Plains Historical Museum,
Search Center Canyon, Texas

– 9 –

The Llano Estacado

Clovis News Journal, May 14, 1946
• *Candidate for Governor Arrested* •
• *Neighboring Quay County Wheat Crop a Failure* •
• *Annual Salvation Army Drive Goal, $9,700* •
• *Dow Jones Average Hits 191* •

After two days of riding cross-country, Jerry and Fan approached the outskirts of Clovis, New Mexico on the Texas border. From the looks of it, spring on the Llano Estacado—the common name for New Mexico's high plains—meant thunderstorms. Huge black clouds blotted out the sun and the wind had a chill to it. Gusting from the northwest it kicked up dust, swirling it into dust devils that danced past them and disappeared into the air. Jerry jammed his hat down and lowered his chin.

Fan worried him. She had been off her feed since the day they left the Palo Duro. That same night Jerry noticed pimple-looking bumps on her back. Over the past two days she had become increasingly lethargic; she now had a runny nose and her breathing seemed labored. Jerry was aware that distemper produced those symptoms and that he needed to get her to a vet fast. He glanced at the sky, suddenly aware that the storm was going to come first, like it or not.

With no warning, Fan halted. Jerry took his worried gaze off the sky and dismounted. Strings of mucus poured from her nose; she was wheezing and her head hung almost to the ground. Heart pounding, he placed his hand on Fan's neck to see if she had a fever. "My God, Fan,

I need to get you help. You're getting worse by the minute!" Jerry flinched as lightning streaked across the black sky and thunder boomed on its heels. The storm was about to cut loose full force and, at this moment, what they needed was shelter. Then, like a prayer answered, he spotted the first buildings he'd seen in two days. "Come on, girl, we've got to make a run for it."

Jerry started running, pulling Fan by her lead rope. She followed reluctantly, needing constant urging to keep moving. As Jerry drew closer he could see that the structure closest to the road was a barn. Its doors opened, and a man just inside was motioning them in. Lightning and thunder crashed simultaneously above them and rain let loose in a cloudburst. Jerry sprinted the last ten yards with Fan now leading the way.

"This looks like a doozy, even by Clovis standards," the man shouted above the storm. "You and your mare better wait this one out inside."

Jerry wiped his face on his sleeve. "Thanks, mister," he shouted back. "Snot's pouring out of my horse's nose. I'm afraid it's distemper."

"Full-blown, I'd say."

"I don't want to infect your animals."

The man waved off Jerry's concern. "I can't let you be out in this storm. I've got a stall away from the others. I'll call my vet. As soon as this blows over you'd best get her into town." A clap of thunder drowned out the rest of his words. He motioned for Jerry to follow. Three horses pranced nervously in their stalls and whinnied as the storm intensified. The rancher led the way to a single stall at the opposite end of the barn, away from the open door. The enclosure had fresh straw covering the floor. The man helped Jerry get Fan inside.

"I really appreciate this," Jerry said. "I'll be sure to clean the stall out before we leave."

"That's okay, son. You've got a pretty sick mare. Soon as you can, you'd better get her to Doc Rivers' place. It's on this road." He indicated the road that ran alongside his property. "I'll have my son burn the straw and wash the bucket out with lye. It's nothing we haven't done plenty of times before."

Jerry removed Fan's saddle and dried her down, then put her blanket back on. She stood listless, her head lowered and her eyes half-closed. The rancher brought a bucket of water and Fan drank a small amount but refused the bran and hay he offered. He told Jerry to make himself at home and then sprinted through the rain to his house to call the vet.

"Don't worry, girl, I'm going to get you help as soon as I can." Jerry bent close and spoke in a calm reassuring voice. He cupped his hand and applied gentle pressure back and forth along the crest of Fan's neck, something she liked as well as being scratched under her chin. She rewarded Jerry with a soft nicker as the thunder crashed directly above them.

The storm raged for two hours and then rumbled off toward Texas. Bright sun took over the afternoon sky, bringing warmth that brought the barn's odors to life: hay, horse dung, and whiffs of damp earth. The rancher came back and opened the barn door. "Doc Rivers is expecting you." Jerry thanked him for his kindness, then leading Fan, walked the two miles into Clovis. Jerry remembered hearing that the Llano Estacado or "staked plains," had been so named because in the early days of settlement there were no trees, no rocks, nothing to mark a traveler's way. Inventive travelers drove stakes in the ground to keep from getting lost.

Now, wheat fields beaten down by the downpour stretched into the distance on both sides of the road. At the edge of Clovis Jerry encountered a neatly trimmed yard with a sign, "James Rivers, DVM." The vet's office, in a barn adjacent to a white clapboard house, had a horseshoe nailed above the door. Doc Rivers came out of his house with a slap of the screen door when Jerry led Fan into the yard. "Woody called me," he said as he shook Jerry's hand. "He said you'd be bringing your mare as soon as the storm blew over. Looks like distemper all right." The vet thoroughly examined Fan, first listening to her heart and lungs with his stethoscope, and then pressing it against her side to listen to her belly. He ran his hands over her flanks and timed her pulse with his watch by pressing his finger behind Fan's left elbow. "Pulse is a little fast. She's got a fever all right." He checked her legs all the way down and then looked at her hooves. "Needs her shoes replaced," he said, matter of factly. Fan didn't fight Doc Rivers when he pulled down her lower jaw and shined a light down her throat. "You are a sick girl, aren't you?" He stroked her muzzle.

Doc Rivers counted out ten large pills. "These are a sulfa-based antibiotic." He opened Fan's mouth and flipped in a pill, then placed his left palm over her nostrils as he stroked the underside of her chin with his right palm. Done in one fast fluid motion, the trick worked: Fan jerked her head upward and the pill went down. "Good girl." he said and repeated the procedure with a second pill. "Because she's as bad as she is, I gave her two pills to hit it hard. You give her one a day, starting this time tomorrow until they're gone." He held up a bucket of water for Fan to drink. "I'm pretty sure we got it in time, but she's one step away from pneumonia and I don't need to tell you what that means."

Jerry told him about their journey.

"From the size of her legs and chest, I'd guess this mare is an Indian pony, a good strong horse. I think she can probably handle the trip if you rest her up—two days minimum. She needs a chance for the medicine to get into her bloodstream and start working, about forty-eight hours. Once it does you can ride her, but be cautious. Rest her as often as you can." Jerry paid the bill and the veterinarian directed him to the Curry County Fairgrounds. "There's only a caretaker there right now getting things ready for Pioneer Days, but you'll find some enclosed stalls." As he said goodbye, Doc Rivers made Jerry promise that if Fan still had any of the symptoms in two days, he would bring her back, no charge. Jerry promised he would.

He had no trouble finding the fairgrounds, a sprawling complex on the southern edge of Clovis. Adjacent to a giant Santa Fe rail yard and adjoining cattle pens, the fairgrounds appeared deserted. The sun had sunk below the horizon and Jerry could see his breath in the cold evening air. The caretaker must have already gone home, but it was evident that someone had recently been there; a bale of straw had been placed in front of each stable door. Jerry led Fan into a stall at the end of a building, then hauled the bale inside and spread straw over the floor. He found a bucket and brought in water. Fan drank a little and then lowered herself down on the straw. Fan never slept lying down. Jerry's heart sunk watching her. He knelt down and stroked her neck.

"Don't die on me, girl. Please don't die," he whispered.

Jerry felt too tired to pace, and too upset and frightened to sleep. He had seen injured and sick horses put down and he wanted no part of that for his valiant mare. He spread his bedroll in the corner of the stall, opened a can of pork and beans, and ate in the waning light, never taking his eyes off his exhausted horse.

He watched her until his eyes grew heavy, then he stretched out with his head propped against Fan's saddle. As the night grew dark, Jerry felt a sick dread creeping over him. Despite the distant sound of cattle lowing and the forlorn whine of a train whistle, Jerry could hear Fan's labored breathing. He fought back tears as he sent a silent prayer heavenward for Fan.

Still farther away, he heard what sounded like church bells.

– 10 –

In the Nick of Time

Clovis News Journal, May 15, 1946
• *French Prime-Minister Pompidou Succeeds DeGaulle* •
• *U of Michigan Cooperates with Johns Hopkins to Build Synchroton,*
300 Million Volt Current Produces Energy •
• *Deadlocked Coal Negotiations Idle 71,000 Miners* •

Morning brought a slight improvement in Fan. She struggled to her feet and Jerry could see the mucus drainage had decreased, but she still wouldn't eat. She did drink two buckets of water, good news because Doc Rivers had told him that, for the first twenty-four hours water was more important than food. After she drank, Fan looked at Jerry with soulful eyes, then went back to sleep, this time standing up. He leaned his forehead against her warm side and ran his hand over her neck. "One of those damned troughs on the other side of Amarillo must have been infected. I promise you, girl, we're not leaving until you're better. I don't want to lose you, bet or no bet."

Jerry heard a knock on the stall door. Ernie, caretaker for the Curry County Fairgrounds, said he noticed the outside bale of hay was gone and wanted to know about the Fair's first guests. "We're not here for the fair. My mare came down with distemper and Doc Rivers suggested I bring her to the fairgrounds to recuperate." Jerry told him about the trip they were on and offered to pay for the straw. His host was as hospitable as the rancher, and would not take Jerry's money. By the looks of his bowed legs, sweat-stained Stetson, and show of concern for Fan, Jerry immediately knew Ernie was a cowboy. He insisted on staying with Fan so Jerry could go in to Clovis to get supplies. "First, let me get her some hay." Ernie returned within a few minutes, a bale of hay balanced on his shoulder.

Fan never ceased to amaze Jerry. She had always been unflappable, a steady horse that wasn't skittish. Still, as sick as she was, she surprised him by not shying or backing away when Ernie came into her stall. He crooned to her in Spanish, first holding out his hand for her to smell and then moving slowly around her stall. He offered a handful of hay. "Try a little of this, *Chiquita mia,*" he said quietly in a sing-song voice. A triumphant smile appeared on his leathery face when Fan began to nibble. "All the ladies love me."

"Well, this one sure does," Jerry said.

Jerry walked into town, stopping on the way to buy a copy of the *Clovis News Journal.* He easily found the restaurant that Ernie said the local cowboys frequented. Jerry read the paper while he waited for his breakfast. He had hardly slept since the Palo Duro, and the previous night had only eaten a can of cold beans. Hungry, sleepy, and worried, Jerry silently tried to regroup as he drank his coffee, telling himself it wasn't his fault that Fan got sick, but admitting he felt guilty because she had.

Being around other people, the rancher, Doctor Rivers, Ernie, and the friendly waitress who kept bringing him coffee, helped lift his spirits. Jerry thought wistfully of Claire Elizabeth Dupree, her pretty smile and how good she smelled. Her image evaporated when the waitress delivered a platter of flapjacks, eggs, and bacon, the fragrant aroma of lavender replaced by maple syrup, bacon, and fresh coffee. Jerry glanced around as he ate.

Ernie had called it right about the restaurant being a cowboy hangout. Most of the customers looked and sounded like cowhands. Jerry overheard stories and jokes about cowboys; they talked about hay crops and horses. They nodded or tipped their hat in his direction as they filed by his booth; they recognized a cowboy when they saw one. Jerry was from Oklahoma; they were from New Mexico but the location didn't matter. They were a fraternity, these lanky, jeans-clad, boot-wearing, weathered men who called themselves cowboys. They shared a way of life, a love of horses, a respect for the land and what they did. They worried and talked about the same things that Jerry talked about with his ranch hands. He didn't know their names yet he felt he was one of them. Their presence and hearing snatches of their conversation improved his disposition as much as the food. Jerry ate every morsel on his plate and paid the bill. He touched the brim of his hat, and each cowboy acknowledged him in return as he exited. Jerry took off through the streets of Clovis in search of a store.

The tracks of the Santa Fe rail yards separated the Curry County Fairgrounds from the town. From the rail yard came a cacophony of sounds: train engines stopping and starting, iron wheels grinding against metal rails, screeches, train whistles, and clanging bells. The cattle pens flooded the air with familiar sounds and smells. The combination of sounds had helped keep Jerry awake the previous night. That and his overwhelming concern for Fan.

Downtown Clovis was ablaze with red, white, and blue banners. Draped across Main Street, they announced the upcoming festivities. "Clovis Pioneer Days June 6-8 Curry County Fairgrounds; Big Rodeo; Barrel Racing; Tractor Pull; Chili Cook-Off; Pie Eating Contest."

A small city, Clovis had a busy downtown section surrounded by tree-lined streets with well-kept houses and yards. And, on almost every corner, a church. On the hour the town became a symphony of ringing bells, blending into a joyful melody from wooden, adobe, and brick towers. Jerry's spirits soared at the clear, pure sounds—a chorus that seemed to say things were going to be okay; Fan had gotten help in the nick of time. Signs of an upcoming celebration, cowboys smiling and nodding their friendly hellos, made Jerry think of Enid and the Cherokee Strip celebration. He had accompanied Rolla and Frank on their two-week Chisholm Trail ride to commemorate Jesse Chisholm's founding of the cattle route. Their ride ended in Enid and, because they were deemed important to the event, Frank and Rolla's arrival helped to signal the beginning of the annual festivities.

Those thoughts led to home and family. It was Tuesday morning. At three o'clock, the tower bell at Pleasant Valley School near Guthrie would ring and Byron, Bill, and David would rush home to do their chores and then probably go fishing. Being Tuesday, Jerry wondered what his mom would be cooking for supper. Sundays she cooked fried chicken. In fact, Sunday supper was *always* fried chicken. Frank and Rolla no doubt had been there and Jerry was sure Frank would have stayed at the Bar R to help Rolla with the summer work in his absence.

But you never knew about Frank Eaton; he never planned anything. Instead, he invited into his life whatever came his way. He always said, "If you don't make a bunch of plans, life'll be full of surprises." Rolla Goodnight maintained there wasn't another human being like Frank Eaton, and he was right. The very thought of the small, wiry man made Jerry smile. Though he was close to his family in Perkins, he and Rolla were never far apart, riding together at the head of parades all through Oklahoma. In the early thirties Frank had helped build the chicken house at the Guthrie place.

Frank gave David his first chew of tobacco (which made him sick) and he gave Jimmy an Indian bow he'd made from orange tree wood. Frank was a gunslinger in the finest tradition and would give you the shirt off his back or the horse out from under him. Generous, impulsive, and fearless, Frank epitomized the gun-toting, fun-loving, story-telling American cowboy. Jerry never tired of hearing his tale about shooting it out with horse thieves that were making off with Owens Cattle Company cattle; he killed three of them and took three bullets in the melee. Frank showed him the scars. "Laid me for up a while." Varmints, thieves, judges, and lawmen—his stories were the stuff of legends and they were true. Like Rolla, Frank loved to recount their adventures with gusto, but he was honest to a fault.

Jerry bought supplies for himself, rolled oats for Fan, and two more horse shoes to use with the two he brought along. He found the

Clovis Post Office at 4th and Mitchell and went in. Jerry knew if his family didn't receive word from him soon, they would get worried. Inside the building, a huge mural depicting men and women hard at work on a variety of WPA projects occupied one wall. Jerry studied it as he waited in line to buy penny post cards. Lots of folks had praised the WPA, Franklin Roosevelt's Works Projects Administration, for the relief it offered during the Great Depression. Rolla had strong opinions about that and politics in general, and would voice them at the slightest provocation.

A life-long Democrat, Rolla parted company with the Democratic president over acreage control on wheat and cotton land. He lambasted Roosevelt at every opportunity over the controls, and anyone within Rolla's earshot soon found it wise to avoid the subject all together. Jerry smiled as he remembered the time his grandfather, brandishing his Winchester, had chased an inspector from the U.S. Department of Agriculture off the Bar R. "You may be from the U.S. Government, mister," he bellowed at the retreating figure, "but you're on U.S. Goodnight property. Now git!"

Jerry arrived back at the fairgrounds in time to give Fan her pill. Ernie said she'd finally eaten a good amount of hay and offered again to watch her any time Jerry needed to go to town. Looping the lead rope around Fan's neck, Jerry led her out of the stall into the warm sun. She lifted her head and sniffed the air. The pills were taking hold; Fan looked better and seemed perkier. Jerry cleaned and trimmed her hooves and replaced all four of Fan's worn shoes.

Her underlying Osage Indian sturdiness proved itself. She bounced back quickly with two and a half days of solid rest, lots of rolled oats, her favorite brand of hay, and good clean water. Jerry gave her the medicine faithfully and led her for a walk around the track three times each day to keep her muscles from stiffening. On the third evening, he let her loose in a fenced-in paddock and he and Ernie watched as Fan tossed her head and pranced. She trotted back and forth along the fence and then rolled in the dirt. Lowering herself down on her right side, she rolled, got up and shook, and then lay down on her left side and did the same thing. She got down and back up a great deal easier than the night they arrived. "Now I know she's feeling better," Jerry said.

A dusty, straw-covered mess, she looked like the Fan he started out with. "You are one sorry-looking lady, and am I ever happy to see you that way." Jerry said. He stood close to the fence and whistled. "Watch this, Ernie." Fan trotted up and stuck her head over the fence close to Jerry's face. He blew into her nostrils. Fan wiggled her muzzle and waited expectantly. Jerry did it again with predictable results. She whinnied, then raised and lowered her head in a giant affirmative nod, curling her top lip up revealing all of her big front teeth. Ernie laughed aloud at her comic expression. She looked as though she was having a good laugh. Fan put her head close, wanting more. "She loves it when I do that." Jerry brushed her off and rode Fan bareback around the track. Her breathing sounded normal; she acted frisky; she seemed ready to go. "I promised you, girl, we'd wait until you were better. Now that you are, we have to get going. We've got a bet to win."

– 11 –

The Rockies

Clovis News Journal Headlines, May 17, 1946
• *Organ Dedicated to War Hero (Church Organ)* •
• *Railroad Workers Killed in Freak Rail Yard Accident* •
• *City Parking Meters "Take" Averages $100 per Day* •

The following morning Ernie wished them luck and watched as they rode away. Jerry and Fan skirted the Santa Fe railroad yards and cattle pens then headed due west across the yucca-studded Llano Estacado—the very name made him sit tall in the saddle. Rolla and Frank had crossed it several times. Charlie Goodnight and Oliver Loving and countless others had crossed the Llano Estacado as well. This country had once been the stomping grounds of Billy the Kid and Butch Cassidy. It was high desert with a cool breeze, prickly cactus, and sage so thick its fragrance filled your senses. Jerry took in the panorama, and suddenly Rolla's reason for the trip became crystal clear, what it was that he wanted Jerry to experience before it disappeared: vistas that filled the senses, miles of wide open country, sky without end—important memories in his grandfather's and Frank's life. It was now his own adventure unfolding and Jerry could easily picture Frank and Rolla as young men and better understand and feel what they experienced.

Straight ahead two days' ride lay Fort Sumner on the banks of the Pecos River, the sight of Billy the Kid's grave. Frank said to be sure to see it, that Pat Garrett, the lawman who had killed Billy, had been a good friend of his. And according to Rolla, Charlie's partner, Oliver

Loving, had died at the fort in 1867 of complications from having his arm amputated. Loving desperately wanted to be buried in his beloved Texas and Charlie, who was with him until the end, promised his friend that his wish would be honored. True to his word, Charlie Goodnight rode back to Ft. Sumner from Texas four months later and had Loving's body exhumed. With a specially-built casket, a large crew of cowboys, and six big mules, he returned his partner's body to Weatherford, Texas for a full Masonic funeral. Charlie told the story with great sadness when young Rolla had asked about Loving's picture hanging on the living room wall at the JA Ranch.

Jerry located Billy the Kid's gravesite near the banks of the Pecos River. The old fort had been preserved, probably looking much like it had in the days of the Kid. An adobe marker in the cemetery stood solidly as the final resting place of one of the West's most famous gunfighters and his two friends. At the top of the marker: the word "Pals, " and underneath: "William H. Bonney, alias Billy the Kid, Died July, 1881." On either side stood the markers of two members of his gang, "Charlie Bowdre and Tom O'Folliard, Died Dec 1880."

Jerry could feel himself reaching back in time, envisioning the world that once belonged to the famous cattle baron, the one that had forged young Rolla Goodnight and Frank Eaton. Standing at the foot of the graves, hand on his Colt .45—Frank's Colt .45—Jerry mentally pictured the thousands of fast-draws he and Frank practiced during the winter. How easy it had become. It must have been easy for the Kid, too. Who taught him? Did he have a Frank Eaton in his life? Frank had laughingly called him "Jerry the Kid" when he finally outdrew him. Ironic that twenty-two-year-old Billy the Kid died the same year Frank rode through here looking for a killer of his own.

Pat Garrett was the law around Albuquerque when Frank caught up with Wyley Campsey in the New Mexico Territory in 1881. Wyley Campsey, wanted for the murder of an officer in the Indian Territory, was the last one alive of the six men who had murdered Frank's father; Frank had already dispatched the other five. Garrett proved to be a good friend; after listening to Frank's story he offered to arrest Campsey to avoid the risk of Frank being killed. Twenty-one years old at the time, Frank Eaton wore a deputy marshal badge on his chest and carried a letter of introduction from Captain Knipe of the Cattlemen's Association.

Frank told Garrett he didn't want Campsey arrested, that his life's mission would never be finished until his father's last murderer was dead. "He or I will hear the cook call breakfast in hell." With Garrett watching from inside the saloon's doors, Frank out-drew Campsey and his two bodyguards on the street outside, killing all three. The last words they heard: "fill your hand, you sonofabitch." Frank was hit in the leg and left arm, and one of his Colt .45s was destroyed in the battle. After the shoot-out, Pat Garrett helped Frank back on his horse, Bowlegs, and sent him to the home of a friend to get patched up and recuperate. Before Frank rode away, Garrett thanked him for getting rid of three bad guys and shoved a Colt .44 with an eight inch barrel into one of Frank's empty holsters. Later, the man who patched Frank up told him how lucky he was to have that particular gun; it was the one Pat Garrett had used to kill Billy the Kid.

Jerry rode four miles north into the town of Ft. Sumner where he replenished his supplies and bought a picture of Billy the Kid for Byron. In a stack of dusty books he found a tattered copy of *The Authentic Life of Billy the Kid by Pat F. Garrett* for Frank. Jerry sat on a bench in front of the post office and wrote a letter to his parents and one to Frank and Rolla. He mailed them with the book and the picture.

As he rode away from Fort Sumner, it occurred to Jerry that Frank hadn't mentioned his trip, only the gunfight itself. But he would have had to cross the Rockies to reach Albuquerque and Wyley Campsey. Frank didn't cross the Continental Divide sixty-five years ago because his trip had ended in Albuquerque. Jerry's route would take him farther south than Frank's, but he carried the same Colt and would cross the same mountains and sleep under the same stars as his mentor and friend. Frank was twenty-one then; Jerry was twenty. It gave Jerry a new perspective. Frank did it; he could surely do it, too.

After a full day's ride west of Fort Sumner the wind swept aside the high cirrus clouds and Jerry got his first real look at the Rocky Mountains, all the way to the top. He slowed Fan, then brought her to a stop and dismounted. Jerry could only stare. Covered by sagebrush and dotted with golden prince's plume and pink desert mallow, the plains stretched into the distance, only ending where the Rockies began. Occasional craggy peaks covered with snow jutted high into the turquoise sky, their sharpness interrupting the flowing silhouette of rounded heights, angular slopes, and vertical shale walls that made up the range. The Rockies filled Jerry's vision as high and as wide as he could see. This obstacle, if such a monument of nature could be called that, had sparked Jerry's initial fear about the ride. Now, alone with Fan and surrounded only by earth and sky, he viewed them with awe. "We're going to cross those, Fan. If we stacked Oklahoma's tallest mountain on top of itself, it still wouldn't be that high."

He kept Fan on a due-west course going cross-country through the upper Sacramento Mountains, part of the range that formed the spine of the Rockies. He stopped to buy grain at a small ranch he happened across; otherwise, rangy longhorns, astonishing vistas, and local wild-life were all he saw. Some coyotes, sitting on an outcropping of rocks, like old folks on their front porch, watched Jerry and Fan pass. Jerry smiled. "Dad didn't want us to make this trip, Fan, but if he could see this, he would understand."

Pungent pine forests gave way to boulder-strewn valleys, only to rise again to pastures ringed by pine and aspen-forested slopes. The color of the sky depended upon the time of day, and ranged from an early morning pale, translucent blue to deep turquoise when the sun reached its zenith. Jerry took extra rests with Fan because of the altitude, well aware of the stress on her lungs. Instead of three times per day, they now stopped five. The terrain called for them to be constantly climbing, then descending, and then climbing again. Fish and game were plentiful; Jerry ate well.

He spotted a herd of wild mustangs across a valley. That same night he heard the powerful, unbeaten call of a wolf affirming his dominance. The long, wailing cry resonated so intensely throughout the still valley, that it raised the hair on the back of Jerry's neck. He held his breath until it died and all was quiet again. Early one morning, he watched silently as a mule deer drank up-wind from the same stream where he washed up. And every day falcons, hawks, and eagles circled overhead, watching from their lofty vantage on the up-drafts and wind currents. On their seventh day out of Clovis, Jerry arrived at a rocky escarpment jutting out of the tall pines. It offered his first panoramic look at what lay ahead.

Visible through a golden haze across a valley below, loomed another range of mountains, the Continental Divide. As impressive as his first view of the Rockies, the mountains at the moment glowed with the colors of the setting sun. Below, the Rio Grande River, deep in the shadows of early evening, ambled from north to south, lazily crooking its way between the two ranges—massive upheavals of Mother Earth millions of years in the making.

Jerry eyed the view, envisioning more rim rock mesas, more timbered hills and mountainous country they would have to cross. "Back home, Fan, I thought I was a cowboy. I wasn't. But I'm pretty sure I will be by the time we get to Hollywood."

– 12 –

The Continental Divide

Socorro Chieftain, May 25, 1946
• *First Polio Case Shows up in Socorro Area* •
• *1½ Million Injured, 16,000 Die Nationwide in 1945 Farm Accidents* •
• *$2 Million in G.I. Loans to New Mexico Vets: Not One Default* •

Jerry and Fan made their way out of the Rockies alongside a stream that led down to the valley below. Once they reached the Rio Grande River they turned south, traveling past newly planted fields of cantaloupes and chili peppers, one field after another of shiny-leafed young plants in rich-looking soil. Early the next morning they reached Socorro, New Mexico.

Once a mining center, it now functioned as a busy business and farming hub sprawled along the western banks of the river. Socorro resembled a picturesque city in old Mexico, laid out in a grid pattern of streets, with stores and warehouses that bespoke of earlier boom times. The Atchison, Topeka, and Santa Fe train depot sat at one end of Manzanares Street and a large central plaza at the other. Jerry followed Manzanares a short distance into town and then turned Fan onto California Street. On the corner, the dark windows of Price-Lowenstein Mercantile told him it was early. Except for the Capitol Bar, a fine old stone building, California Street held a mixture of sagging adobe buildings with fancy brick eaves, and worn wooden structures that long ago were no-doubt considered grand.

There were scant few cars parked in front of the stores, but those early Socorro citizens who were out shopping stopped and stared at him with his collar-length hair, all-black clothes, and a tie-down holster with a Colt in it. As he rode his strutting pinto down California Street, Jerry admitted he must have looked like an outlaw right out of a western movie, for a pretty little black-haired girl about five years old pointed at him and spoke excitedly to her mother. "*Mira, Mama. Mira el bandito!*" She peeked out from behind her mother's skirts. He touched the brim of his hat as he reined Fan up in front of a mercantile store whose clerk was just opening its doors.

The clerk at J. L. Grimes Store spoke very little English; Jerry spoke even less Spanish. There were no other customers and the young *señorita* tried desperately to help. He searched for a tube of Ipana toothpaste but could not find it and had no idea how to ask. Finally Jerry mimed squeezing toothpaste onto an imaginary brush, brushing his teeth, and then ended his pantomime with a big smile. "Ah, *Señor, pasta dentífricia.*" After much giggling, she produced the toothpaste from behind the counter; it cost twenty cents. He bought oats for Fan, but didn't even try to find Unguentine, the ointment he needed for his sun and wind-burned face. As he exited the store, Jerry ran smack into the Socorro law.

"Good morning. Mind if I ask what you're doing carrying a gun?" His name was Alfredo Baca and he identified himself as Chief of Socorro Police. Chief Baca explained that Grimes Mercantile had been robbed twice in the last six months, as had the drugstore, the post office, and the Sprouse-Reitz store. He was more than a little curious about a shaggy-haired young man, armed with a Colt, and riding through his town. Jerry told him about the trip they were on and presented the receipt for the supplies and feed he had just bought.

Captain Baca apologized for his interrogation and walked with Jerry back to Fan's side. "Good-looking pinto," he said. Fan strained forward as Jerry approached. She knew by now that when he walked toward her with a gunny sack, she would shortly get a taste of rolled oats. Jerry held the sack open; Fan stuck her nose in and began chomping.

"A good-looking and hungry pinto. *Vaya con Dios, mi amigo,*" Captain Baca said as Jerry rode away.

Fan was eating good again. Jerry carried four to five days' supply of grain, about twenty-five pounds, protein food, an important fuel. She ate grass at every opportunity and liked the occasional hay that Jerry had been able to get for her on the trip. Still, when he tightened her cinch he could tell Fan had lost weight. But, then, he had, too; Jerry had to tighten his own belt.

Jerry followed the general direction of Highway 60 due west from Socorro. Machines and crews were busy at work on the old two-lane road at the base of the mountain. Jerry did not own a car and, even if he could afford the $1,125 price tag for a new one, they were as scarce as new housing. The war had consumed the country's raw materials, and according to radio and newspapers, it would be two years before production would make them readily available. The word *progress* flicked through Jerry's mind.

Jerry and Fan traveled in a straight line up the eastern slopes of the Continental Divide. They seldom intersected the curving highway that ambled its way around thickly forested mountain peaks. He stopped to rest Fan in Magdalena, a village sprawled in the sun at the base of Lady Magdalena Mountain. This was cattle and sheep country and Magdalena served as its center. Gangly cowboys, dark-skinned Indians, and a fair number of eastern tourists trying to look like westerners ambled in and out of the hotel, the post office, and the train station. Magdalena stood at the end of a spur railroad line. Railcars parked on the tracks with their doors opened to adjoining rows of connecting pens, were being loaded, some with bawling cattle, others with sheep. It was shipment time, a time Jerry knew well. The climb was gradual but constant and the surroundings dramatic. From a trail that led between ten-thousand foot forested peaks, Jerry and Fan entered the Plains of San Augustin, an ancient concave lake bed ringed in the far distance by more towering mountains.

It was a wild, rugged country of one spectacular vista after another.

Jerry and Fan passed cattle herds being driven to the rail yard in Magdalena. The cowboys accompanying them offered a friendly wave. Sheep bunched in tight flocks as their Basque sheepherders kept them moving briskly along, kept a respectful distance from the longhorns. Jerry made camp near the tiny town of Datil, along the southeastern rim of the plains.

Mountainside slopes that received sunlight were thick with pinions and junipers, while the shady hillsides were covered with conifers. At five the following afternoon, warm sunlight gave way to dark skies and a chill-to-the-bone wind that blew straight at them. Jerry would have liked to ride for another two hours, but the threatening skies and eight thousand foot elevation changed his mind. He rode a half mile off the highway and found a protected spot to camp.

Jerry donned his rain slicker and picketed Fan near a wall of granite boulders. A near-by grove of pinion trees would provide a canopy if it snowed, and snow looked imminent. He unpacked his gear, watered and fed Fan, then got a fire going. As he looked around at his camp Jerry congratulated himself for his choice of sites. The wall of boulders would reflect the fire's heat and protect them from the wind. The coming storm wasn't nearly as worrisome now.

An hour of daylight remained and Jerry intended to use it to bag his dinner. Grabbing his Winchester, he hiked ten minutes in a straight line due north from camp until he came to the edge of a meadow. He crouched down and waited to see what would appear. A faint honking sound high above made him look up, a formation of Canada geese heading south. They were out of range, but Jerry acknowledged he wouldn't have shot one anyway—to do so would create a space in that perfect V formation. Thirty minutes went by. Jerry had almost resigned himself to eating beans when three grouse flew out of the woods and landed in the meadow. He bagged one with his first shot.

Jerry usually hunted or fished four days out of seven, even more in the mountains where small game was plentiful. He could gut, skin, flour, and prepare any game in fifteen minutes flat, a long-ago lesson learned from his father. Jerry built a spit and spent the next hour turning the bird until it was a golden brown.

Snow started falling just as he finished his meal. Not snow flurries like they'd experienced in the Rockies, but a wind-driven, blinding snow that blanketed trees and rocks and coated everything vertical and horizontal. Within an hour four inches had fallen in camp and more could be seen out away from the rocks. The snow gave Jerry an eerie feeling, boxing him in, obscuring distance and perspective, cutting off all sound with its insulation. He knew if it snowed hard all night and the wind kept up, they would have a difficult time getting through the snowdrifts.

There hadn't been any car lights since he made camp. The only sounds were the crackling fire and howling wind, which made Fan nervous. She was used to Oklahoma winds—which this was not—and she didn't like snow at all. Tense and fidgety, she shook her head, switched her tail abruptly, and kept shifting directions. Jerry got up and brushed the snow off her. He cupped his hand and massaged along the ridge of her neck.

"Hey, this is just a little snow. Don't worry," he crooned. His voice seemed to settle her. Jerry huddled by the fire and tried to think about the following day. His rational mind told him that Pietown was only eight miles ahead; his emotional mind insisted he and Fan were totally alone on the mountain top. Nervous, Jerry busied himself gathering dry wood from under low-hanging branches. He stacked it against the rocks. "I've got to make sure to wake up and keep the fire going," Jerry said in Fan's direction.

He covered his bedroll with his rain slicker and then added a few pieces of pinion to the fire. The resinous wood sizzled and spit, sending forth heat and quick spikes of flame. Knowing Fan would need water to drink in the morning, he heaped snow in the bucket and placed it at the edge of the fire.

Light replaced darkness and Jerry awoke the next morning to a terrible smell. He opened his eyes with a start and gazed directly into

Fan's yellow teeth. She nuzzled his cheek. "Fan!" Jerry let out a startled holler. "For cryin' out loud, your breath smells awful." He jumped up and stood shivering on top of his snow-covered bedroll.

It had stopped snowing. Still, as protected as it was, his camp was buried under a foot of snow. He figured the two mounds near his bedroll had to be cowboy boots. Jerry dumped the snow out of them, pulled them on, and then removed the snow from his bedroll. Everything he touched was wet and ice cold. He had a hard time finding his hat. The fire had burned out long before he awoke and the remaining wood stuck out of the snow just far enough for him to find it. Fan looked like a four-legged snowman. And the water in the bucket had a one inch layer of solid ice on top.

"Dammitall, Fan, if you wanted to wake me, why didn't you do it in the middle of the night?" Jerry stomped out away from Fan and stood under a pinion tree, its branches loaded with snow. He looked back at his sorry camp. "Damn it all." he roared and threw up his arms in disgust. The sharp sound dislodged the snow. It landed squarely on Jerry's uncovered head, forming a cone on top and creating peaks on his nose, eyelashes, and shoulders. He could hardly see. It slid down his collar and made icy streams down his back. Jerry brushed it off his face and saw Fan watching him, flicking her ears back and forth.

Now he was disgusted and wet. "I said dammitall," Jerry shouted again and shook himself. Fan whinnied. "I get the impression you think this is funny."

Maybe Fan shook her head trying to get the snow off, or perhaps her muzzle itched and that's why she wiggled it, showing her big teeth. But to Jerry it looked like she was having a good laugh, a "yup, serves you right" kind of look. "Before you go laughing at me, missy, you should see yourself. You don't look much better."

Jerry dug out his hat and rebuilt the fire. He cleaned the snow off Fan and shook out her blanket. The water in the bucket finally thawed enough to get coffee going. Fan stood with her head over his shoulder next to his face as he squatted by the fire. She wanted water. "Okay, you don't want to drink ice water. Let me fix this, will you?" Fan got her water and grain. Jerry dunked his cold biscuits in hot coffee and ate two half-frozen eggs that he fried to thaw them.

By late morning they made their way back to the highway. The main part of the front had moved east. A few scattered clouds remained, blocking the sun and making the forest look cold, white, and unforgiving. Thirty minutes later the sun popped out and Jerry immediately felt its warmth. The snow-laden trees suddenly became a kaleidoscope of flashing lights and colors, dazzling and brilliant, like being in the midst of a sparkly Christmas card.

The top layer of snow on the highway had blown away with the wind. Fan, not sure of her footing, moved slowly through the eight inches that remained, suspicious of every step. Jerry walked ahead until she was wading through it with no hesitation. When he felt satisfied the road beneath the snow was smooth and even, Jerry mounted up. The last thing he wanted was a leg injury to Fan. She walked confidently along the vacant highway in fresh powder that was half-way up her forearm. Jerry patted Fan's neck. "The worst is over, girl. We'll be out of the snow soon. Things are going to get better now."

– 13 –

Seven Thousand Feet and Climbing

The Socorro Chieftain, May 26, 1946
• *Rotarians Hear Of Freezing Food for Preservation* •
• *Magdalena Stockyards Gear Up For Cattle, Sheep, Rail Shipments* •
• *Reports of Diphtheria Cancel Datil Fiesta* •
• *Wheat Shortage Drives Bread Prices to Dime A Loaf* •

The constant strain because of the altitude began to show on Fan. Except for the two days they'd camped along the Rio Grande, they had been above seven thousand feet and as high as ten thousand for ten days. Lathered and breathing hard, she walked with a slow, plodding step. Jerry dismounted and walked in front. He kept up a steady stream of conversation, partly to encourage Fan, partly to keep himself from worrying. "Come on, you water-guzzlin', hay-eatin' machine. We can't let this mountain lick us." Fan snorted and Jerry chuckled, certain she was letting him know she didn't appreciate his unflattering description. "Okay, okay, I take back what I said."

The day grew hot under the bright sun. A great clump of snow released from a nearby pine with a *thrump*, startling Fan. "At least it didn't land on my head or yours." Another clump fell, and another, echoing like muted dominoes falling in the stillness. Jerry wet his lips and whistled "Cool, Clear Water," a Sons of the Pioneers song. He looked back. Fan held her head higher; she looked alert, switching her tail as though irritated. "Okay, so I can't carry a tune." Jerry alternately whistled and talked until his mouth got too dry to do either. When they reached Pietown near the top of the Divide, Jerry paused to catch his breath and let his heartbeat slow. At over eight thousand feet, the thin crystalline air made getting enough oxygen difficult, but it afforded a spectacular view; pure white snow, a forest of blue-green trees, all of it set against a cloudless turquoise sky.

Pietown, however, had seen better days. It was nothing more than a few sad-looking buildings with its busiest business a ramshackle restaurant that advertised home-made pies. Jerry could see people through the fogged-up windows. In front of the building, two tethered horses slept in the sun; next to them was an old buckboard with two mules hitched to it. He would love a piece of pie, but decided that the quicker they could leave this altitude, the better. As soon as Jerry caught his breath he and Fan moved on, leaving Pietown behind. Three miles later they crested the Divide.

When Fan's breathing slowed, he climbed into the saddle. "Okay, girl. We'll get as far west of Quemado as daylight will allow, then I'm gonna find you a big patch of grama grass and a nice stream." Around them, the snow was melting fast and the westward down slope of the Divide was gentle enough to make the going considerably easier. Jerry let Fan pick her own speed, and she chose the running walk that was responsible for her name.

Late afternoon brought them to Quemado near the western edge of the San Francisco River. The old village, with a small plaza surrounding it, sat in a valley two thousand feet below the summit. Three once-fine buildings constructed of cut stone faced the highway; all the other structures he saw were adobe, made drab by a layer of gray limestone wash. The remainder of Quemado consisted of rutted, dirt side streets with a few tidy houses. Most houses, however, were in various states of disrepair. Some streets he passed ended into nothingness several blocks off the highway. At the end of one, Jerry spotted a sheet-less covered wagon, its exposed rusted stays resembling the ribs of a long-dead creature. The people looked like none he had ever seen—short, dark-skinned, with blue-black hair. Could they be gypsies? Women, dressed in once-bright layered skirts and faded blouses, walked past unsmiling, leading scantily-dressed children by the hand. The men, most of them wearing balloon-legged pants with wide belts and worn vests, stared back at Jerry with open curiosity as he rode by. They didn't look like any cowboys he had ever seen.

Quemado's Country Store had to be the biggest building in town. The size of a warehouse, it had two ancient gas pumps in front. Inside, the majority of the space had been blocked off, leaving only a small front section for the dusty, cluttered collection of goods. Grimy windows let in little of the bright sun outside. The store smelled of grain, coal oil, and sweaty unwashed bodies. The minute he walked in, Jerry experienced a disquieting feeling. Several customers glanced his way; none of them acknowledged him. He noticed immediately the gypsy-looking people spoke a language different than Spanish. And no one spoke English.

Buying supplies on the trip had been something Jerry enjoyed. It gave him a chance to visit with people and learn about the area, even if his host turned out to be the local sheriff. These people eyed him suspiciously, with not a smile among them. He gathered up his supplies and piled them on the counter. The sound of laughter made him look up; it didn't fit. Three men brushed close by and Jerry knew instantly the source of the foul smell. Their clothes and conduct stamped them as outsiders passing through, not locals. They kept their conversation and laughter between themselves and did not include the clerk—no familiarity at all. And it wasn't happy laughter born of humor or amusement, but something different. Whatever the reason, it pricked the hair on the back of Jerry's neck. When he looked their way, all three men averted their eyes. Jerry quickly pointed to a barrel of bran and nodded to the clerk who walked over and began scooping some into a gunny sack. When the clerk had sacked enough, Jerry nodded again. He paid for his supplies and exited without ever having said a word.

Jerry and Fan made a quick exit from Quemado, for the first time on their trip with Jerry unable to shake his uneasy feeling. On the outskirts, they passed a series of inter-connected pens, some with rangy-looking longhorns in them, others with sheep. The vaqueros working in the pens stopped and stared as they passed. As soon as they were beyond the pens, Jerry slowed Fan to a walk. He thought about hospitable Ernie and the friendly cowboys in the Clovis café. *So much for visiting with the locals.*

– 14 –

Everything I Learned Comes Down to This

The Socorro Chieftain, May 30, 1946
• *Magdalena Horse Beats Out Texas Entry in 2 Day Event* •
• *First Geophysics Course in Nation Added by Socorro's*
New Mexico School of Mines •
• *Plans for Tuberculosis Hospital Expansion Okayed* •

Whoever said that New Mexico skies were enchanted was right. No wonder, at this altitude they're halfway to heaven, Jerry thought. The night sky, the darkest blue imaginable, was awash with millions of stars and presided over by a sliver of yellow moon. A sight beyond description, Jerry decided it was the heavenly equivalent of the Texas panhandle and the Llano Estacado rolled into one.

He made camp a half-mile off the highway, not far from the base of a hill scattered with granite boulders big enough to be called mountains themselves. A stream that ran along the base of the hill delivered its melted snow westward, a sure sign they had crossed the Divide. It was cold but clear, unlike "Continental Divide Night," the previous night's blizzard that Jerry swore to forever remember by that name.

After supper Jerry drank his coffee and looked over his map. He marked off the previous days on his calendar; it was May 30, fourteen days since they had ridden into Clovis on the heels of a storm. Two weeks to cross the entire state of New Mexico though, two and a half of those days Fan had spent down with distemper. Already a dozen miles west of Quemado, tomorrow they would reach Arizona. Jerry sipped his coffee, reflecting on the trip. Frank and Rolla had camped on trails like this and no doubt marveled at these same stars. The only difference was they were dogging a couple thousand head of "the dumbest animals God ever created" (one of Frank's many sayings).

"This is different than any trail drive Frank and Grandpa were ever on," Jerry said in Fan's direction. "With a herd, a remuda, a cook, and a chuck wagon plus a crew of cowboys, they had no reason to be lonesome." The fire burned low. Jerry added some wood and glanced at Fan. "Grandpa and Frank had lots of people to depend on if something went wrong, and someone besides their horse to talk to." He looked Fan's way; she hadn't missed a bite. "Are you listening?" Still no response. "I give up on you."

A coyote howled. These mountains were coyote country; Jerry had spotted packs of them during the day. Every night one would begin to howl, like now, and then quickly be joined by a host of others, all together sounding like tormented cries from hell. By comparison, the hoot owl's call from a nearby tree sounded sweet. In between their howls, Jerry heard sounds he'd grown to know. Wind whistled through the tall pines. The campfire snapped and popped, adding its rhythm to Mother Nature's primitive song—reassuring, familiar sounds that signaled the end of another day on the trail.

Jerry appreciated the fire. After night settled, it was a cowboy's savior, comfort and succor for a solitary soul. He looked up in surprise. Fan had moved closer, with sprigs of grass sticking out at all angles from her mouth. "What's the matter? I thought you'd be munching away half the night out there. Coyotes making you nervous?" Fan went right to the spot where Jerry had dumped her rolled oats. She delicately scoured the dirt with her muzzle picking up every last morsel. He chuckled. "I shouldn't complain about how much you eat. You're what got me this far." Jerry stretched out on top of his bedroll, his head propped against Fan's saddle. "We've just about done it, girl, crossed these mountains that worried me so much."

He closed his eyes not yet ready to sleep, savoring new feelings—anticipation and accomplishment, a dose of confidence.

Suddenly, Jerry sat straight up on his bedroll, a sixth sense streaking a chill across his shoulders. *Movement. Something or someone.* He rose, and with the efficient movements of a seasoned cowboy, made a few adjustments to his camp. Jerry grabbed his Winchester, took a last look around the campsite, and then disappeared silently into the darkness. Away from the campfire, his all-black clothes helped him blend into the night.

He listened carefully. *Three sets of footsteps.* The footfalls told Jerry that three men had fanned out in a circle and were sneaking up on his camp from the northwest. A cold, biting wind of ten or fifteen miles an hour whipped steady from the same direction, carrying the sound of branches breaking and boots landing softly on rock-strewn ground.

He tucked his six-foot frame behind an outcropping of granite boulders that separated his campsite from the nearby creek. The boulders' gritty solid surface, icy against his shoulder, would be an impenetrable shield against bullets. Jerry glanced around toward the creek in back of him and then scanned in every direction, searching the night for a moving shape. *Nothing.*

Jerry's hiding spot offered a good view of the campfire. Fanned by the strong breeze, the sap-filled wood burst into flame, bright-hot and hissing, sending blue-tipped, orange tendrils into the air. Away from the heat, the intense cold stung his face, clean-shaven and still warm from the fire. Without his hat, his collar-length hair offered little protection against the biting cold. Jerry's Stetson was in camp, lying askew on his bedroll as though in panic he had thrown it down and fled. His coffee mug and supper plate lay upside down in the dirt. The skillet and his utensils he tossed haphazardly near the fire to reinforce that impression. It was important to make whoever was out there think they had frightened him off.

At the first noise Fan had stopped grazing and raised her head, ears

forward in a study of alertness and fear. Jerry could hear her pawing
and whinnying, struggling against her restraint. There hadn't been time
to check the picket rope; he prayed it would hold. He forced himself to
breathe evenly, remembering the warnings and lessons his grandfather
and Frank had drummed into him: *You gotta have eyes in the back of
your head. Trust your instincts. Pay attention to footsteps. They'll tell
you how many, the direction, and how fast they're comin'. Always
keep your head. Be as cool as the gun you're holdin'.*

Jerry looked heavenward and said silent thanks for his training at
the hands of two of Oklahoma's most experienced cowboys. His trail
skills had been honed razor-sharp by his grandfather, his fast draw
quick as lightning, sharpened by Frank Eaton. No better teacher
existed, a man so good and so fast he'd earned the nickname Pistol
Pete and, at seventeen, been sworn in as a Deputy Marshal by Isaac
Parker, the hanging judge.

Jerry's eyes searched the darkness; the footsteps were close now.
Three shadowy figures emerged from the trees. They leapt into the
firelight, sweeping pistols and rifles from side to side in front of them.
Their astonished expressions and abrupt movements told Jerry they
had expected to surprise their victim. Jerry squinted. *The guys from
the store!*

They were a desperate-looking lot. One of them, about his own
age, looked short and stocky and had a holster strapped low on his
hips, the pistol drawn. The second man had a scruffy beard, wore no
hat, and carried a rifle. He looked wild and mean. The third man
appeared older, with a slack belly that threatened to explode the
buttons from his shirt. His eyes darting around camp, the older man
moved his rifle back and forth in a half-circle and peered into the
darkness in Jerry's direction. Despite the cold, sweat glistened on the
fat thief's forehead below the tattered sombrero pushed back on his
head.

Jerry pulled back and held his breath. He heard muffled voices
speaking rapid Spanish. Exhaling slowly, Jerry leaned forward. The

young thief flipped Jerry's dinner plate upright with the toe of his boot and said something. The older man laughed and set his rifle down against a pine tree. He lifted the edge of his vest to wipe his brow and Jerry spotted a knife handle protruding from a leather holder attached to his belt. Six inches long, the knife's sheath told Jerry they meant business.

The young stocky thief's posture relaxed; he returned the six-shooter to his holster. Their mean-looking companion tossed his Winchester down on the bedroll, its barrel landing with a smack against Fan's saddle. He picked up Jerry's Stetson and placed it on his head. *"Que bueno."* That much Spanish Jerry understood. The thought of some no-good thief wearing his hat that he'd paid a week's wages for made Jerry grit his teeth; he fought the urge to rush them. "Hang on," he mouthed silently. Jerry tried to slow his breathing; his heart was thumping like a war drum. Every muscle in his body felt taut, ready to spring. Frank's Colt .45, all six chambers filled, sat cradled loosely in his tie-down holster. Jerry's forefinger sought the notch carved in the Colt handle.

Frank had carved that notch at age seventeen after he killed Shannon Campsey, one-sixth of the Campsey-Ferber gang that had murdered his father when Frank was seven years old. Five more notches carved farther down stood for the rest of the killers, their last vision had been of Frank's smoking Colt.

Jerry held his Winchester cocked and ready in his left hand. The thieves conversed again and then laughed—a sinister laugh that spoke volumes more that their unintelligible words could not. A shiver crept up Jerry's spine as he heard Fan's whinny. When the man with the sombrero moved toward the pinto, Jerry's resolve to be cool evaporated like his breath in the frosty air.

He covered the ten feet to the edge of the camp in a low crouch and lunged into the fire light. The three thieves froze. Jerry's right hand rested lightly on the Colt, still in his holster. With his left hand, he aimed the rifle square at the fat man's sweating forehead.

"Don't touch my horse," he said in a low, threatening voice. Jerry's right hand lifted imperceptibly off the Colt, his fingers moving slightly. "You. Toss my hat back on the bedroll, nice and slow. Now!"

The desperado reached up and removed the Stetson. As he dropped it, the stocky thief used the diversion to go for his holstered pistol. The fat man made a move for his knife. Lightning fast, Jerry drew his Colt and fired.

"Fill your hand, you sonofabitch!" The words came out automatically; the fury and fierceness in his voice surprising him. The pistol flew out of the young thief's hand, fragments of it exploding in every direction. He screamed, dropped to his knees, and grabbed his bloodied hand. Jerry's second shot ripped the fat man's frayed sombrero from his head. Eyes wide with terror, the man sucked in his breath, his fingers frozen on the handle of his knife. Jerry nodded at the sheathed weapon. With slow, deliberate movements the fat man removed his fingers from the knife and raised both hands above his head. Almost as a reflex, his eyes darted down at his rifle still against the tree. Jerry fired a third shot. The rifle split in half, the bullet rendering a gash in the pine tree where it had stood. A fourth shot disintegrated the rifle, sending pieces of it flying through the air.

The man on his knees stopped rocking, his cries suspended in midair. "Get up," Jerry shouted. The injured man struggled to his feet, wiped his face with the sleeve of his good arm, and stood staring at the Colt Jerry had pointing in his direction. All three men stood silent, waiting. Their expressions said they had intended to kill him and now that the tables were turned, they fully expected to die.

"Everything I learned comes down to this," Jerry said, looking at them.

The fat man spoke with a thick accent, exhaling as he did. "Please, *señor,* don't kill us."

"So you sorry bastards speak English after all." Jerry didn't move. "Make no mistake, if I had wanted to kill you, you'd already be dead."

"Si, we made a big mistake. *Por favor—"*

"You're damned right you made a mistake. I hear like a wolf and I see like a hawk. And the only man faster than me with a gun is in Oklahoma. You'd better get your friend some help." Jerry nodded at the injured man. "And don't think of coming back. It would be your last mistake. Understand?" The thief hesitated. Jerry fired his fifth shot into the ground at the man's feet.

The fat man turned on his heel and took off in the dark, the other two right behind him. Jerry heard them crashing through the thick brush, grunting and shouting, panic fueling their flight—boots pounding hard earth in terrified retreat. Jerry moved close to Fan and stood with his hand on her withers, his ear cocked in the direction of the diminishing sounds. Far in the distance he heard a car motor grind, crank to life, and roar off. Then it, too, was gone. Suddenly it was quiet, a quiet so intense that Jerry could hear his heart thudding in his chest, hear his own breathing, uneven and fast. He didn't know whether to laugh, to shake with fear, or shout at the top of his lungs. Refilling the chambers of his Colt, Jerry made his way through the brush and trees, following after the thieves until he could see the highway. Nothing but darkness and silence. Not even the coyotes dared make a sound. He holstered his gun and returned to camp. Jerry stood at the edge of darkness, his heart refusing to slow.

On fire with a feeling he could not name, Jerry stared hard at the sky. From deep inside, instinctive and irrepressible came emotion clawing and fighting its way to the surface. Around and through restraint and vigilance, it struggled for expression. Jerry threw back his head and howled at the stars. He howled long and high like the wolf. Closing his eyes, he did it again. And again.

Jerry howled a triumphant, victorious, long-wailing cry over mountains that reached halfway to heaven, over endless country, fear and loneliness, over men who used darkness—men who would kill for a horse and a hat.

Fan whinnied; he could hear her struggling. Jerry stopped. She was as frightened of him as she had been of the three men. He drew a deep breath and went to Fan, stroking her forehead. He rubbed down between her frightened eyes and stroked her soft muzzle.

"It's okay, girl, it's okay," he said softly. "There's nothing to be afraid of. Nothing ever again."

– 15 –

Sleepin' on the Job

The Socorro Chieftain, May 31, 1946
• *Materials Shortage Holds up Construction of
21 New State Post Office Buildings* •
• *Socorro Police Chief Baca & Son Injured in Auto Accident* •
• *Hwy 60 Construction Leaves 35 Unpaved Miles to Arizona Border* •

Jerry found it impossible to fall asleep after the desperados fled. He jumped at every sound and dozed off once, only to awaken suddenly and find himself sitting up with his gun drawn. Using the fire's light he packed up his camp, and as soon as daylight appeared, he and Fan got underway. The adrenaline released by the run-in with the thieves, coupled with the lack of sleep, took its toll. With the late afternoon sun warm on his chest, Jerry fought to keep his eyes open, but lost the battle. He released the reins and they went slack. On her own, Fan slowed to a rhythmic, rocking walk. Jerry's head drooped, chin on his chest; finally he fell sound asleep in the saddle.

Later, when Fan tired and came to a halt, Jerry woke up. The sun had already set; it was getting dark fast. "What the hell? Where are we?" He dismounted quickly and looked around. Fan immediately began searching for something to eat.

They were in a flat-bottomed draw about thirty feet wide with boulders on both sides; sparse dry grass grew along the outer edges. A few red cedars, dead long ago, stood with bleached branches pointing in every direction like ghostly stick figures. Jerry picketed Fan on a fifteen-foot length of rope to a thick tree trunk near the rocks. "You must be starving. And thirsty. You're used to being fed and watered three times a day."

Fully awake now, Jerry scrambled, realizing he had no more than twenty minutes of light, not enough time to find them a better camp. He poured out a full measure of grain for Fan and hurriedly gathered up slash around the base of nearby trees. With the addition of dead branches and some tenacious prodding, the fire started. Dark had settled in by the time Fan finished off her pile of grain and came looking for water. Jerry poured all but a few cups of water from his canteen into the bucket and she emptied it quickly. "I'm sorry, girl. That's all there is. We'll have to find water first thing in the morning."

Jerry used the rest of the water to make coffee; he desperately needed something hot to drink. He couldn't see to hunt and he shuddered at the thought of beans for supper. Instead, he opened a can of peaches and ate them, anything to stop his rumbling stomach. The fire burned down quickly; it needed leaves, pine cones, anything flammable in order to survive until morning. Searching as far as the fire's waning light would reach, he gathered all the wood he could find and fed the fire until it blazed hot again. He checked to make sure Fan was tethered securely, and then spread his bedroll close to the rocks and climbed in. Despite having slept in the saddle, he fell asleep immediately.

When the ground began to rumble Jerry did not awaken, instead incorporating the unfamiliar noise into his dream. It was when the earth beneath him started shaking and the rumbling grew louder that he awoke with a start. Disoriented, his heart pounding, Jerry grabbed his hat, scrambled out of his bedroll, and jammed his feet in his boots. "Fan," he screamed, his voice lost in the great roar that enveloped them. A solid black mass—stampeding mustangs with heads tossed high and tails flying—raced past flank to flank. Inches away hooves pounded, their noise exploding like thunder in his ears. "Heeyyahh!" Jerry hollered. "Heeyyahh!" he screamed as the mustangs surged closer, slamming him against the rocks. The heat of their bodies, their panicked breathing and excited whinnies flowed so close that Jerry felt a part of it. Their sheer power threatened to pull him in.

The herd thundered through the fire, throwing sparks up into the air, creating a choking, blinding cloud of ashes that engulfed the draw. The mustangs called to Fan and she called back. "Heeyyahh!" Jerry waved his hat and shouted as loud as he could. He swung his arms and kept hollering until the smoke and dust overwhelmed him, and he could holler no more. Then as suddenly as they had come, they were gone.

The sound of their retreating hooves diminished quickly, leaving only the choking haze as evidence of their brief, violent appearance. Dazed and coughing, Jerry discovered he was standing on his bedroll, legs trembling and unable to move; he stared into the darkness after the horses. Fan's whinnies and the sound of her rearing and kicking told him she hadn't gotten away. He stumbled toward her, staying well away from her flying hooves. He used the sharp command he'd practiced with her in Oklahoma. "Quit, Fan, quit!" She whinnied loudly, still prancing and rearing.

Jerry removed Fan's picket rope from the tree, wound it around his hand and held tight. This time he tried the reprimand in a softer, calmer voice. "Easy, Fan, it's me. Come on, girl, settle down." Slowly reeling in her rope, Jerry spoke softly as he inched closer. She whinnied and snorted and tossed her head. He applied a downward pressure on the rope and kept speaking softly, stroking Fan's neck until she calmed down.

"Easy, girl, you don't want to go with them." Jerry ran his hand down her shoulder and front leg; it was trembling as bad as his own. "Like hell you don't." He kept his hand on Fan's flank, and when he felt her relax, he relaxed. Jerry pulled a wooden match from his pocket and struck it on a nearby rock. He shook out his bedroll then spread it out next to the boulder; there was nothing he could do until daylight, so he climbed back in. A last look around revealed only a few remnant embers of the fire. The mustangs had obliterated it and the night was once again pitch black. The air began to clear and Jerry's heartbeat finally slowed. He had no idea where they were or what had happened to his Stetson.

When he opened one eye the next morning, the sun and Fan were already up. Fan stood over him, nudging his shoulder and nickering for him to get up. Jerry opened his other eye. "Some welcoming party your friends gave us last night." He got up and pulled on his boots. Not a trace of last night's fire remained, no black earth where it had been, no evidence of it at all.

Jerry noticed the hollowed-out path in the middle of the draw where the earth had been pulverized to a fine powder by pounding hooves. Why did the herd of wild horses pick this particular path? Jerry followed it down and around a bend; fifty yards ahead he discovered the reason. At the end of the well-traveled path, the land leveled out and led directly into a small lake. "Well, if that doesn't beat all." He walked back up to Fan. She was waiting for him with her ears perked forward, straining against her rope. "You stopped right in the middle of a major mustang highway, missy." Something caught Jerry's eye. Smashed in the dirt up against the rocks, lay the remnants of his Stetson, the hat he paid thirty-five hard-earned dollars for when he got out of the navy. What remained no longer resembled a Stetson. Stomped and shredded, it now contained more dirt than fabric. "This thing wouldn't do to put on a scarecrow.

Jerry looked down at his clothes. He looked almost as bad. "Okay, I know where you can drink your fill and we can wash off this dirt. And I'm telling you right now, lady, that's the last time I fall asleep in the saddle and let *you* pick our campsite."

– 16 –

Civilization at Last

Apache County Independent News, June 1, 1946
* *Truman Creates Central Intelligence Agency* *
* *Springerville Man Wins Magdalena Calf-Roping Event* *
* *Care Packages Provide Basics to War-Ravaged Europeans* *

Jerry discovered that Fan did well on her impromptu navigation. She had maintained a westerly heading, finally coming to a stop a mile off the highway that led to Springerville, Arizona. They backtracked to the highway and headed due west. Fifteen miles later they reached the outskirts of their first Arizona town. After all that happened, Jerry felt like kissing the ground when he saw signs of civilization.

He spotted the water tower first, then several church spires rising from the town's skyline. Visible rows of evenly spaced round tree tops told him that people had planted shade trees. Jerry saw something else, though he rubbed his eyes in disbelief at what he saw. Up ahead was a huge statue at the edge of the road, something that looked like it belonged in a museum. Jerry rode up, dismounted, and could only stare.

On top of a base as tall as he, was the statue of a young woman in flowing dress and wearing a bonnet on her head. She had a baby in her arms and a youngster clinging to her skirts. In weathered bronze, her face glowed in soft patina, beautiful and strong and gentle at the same time; she looked to be about his age. The young woman had no doubt been through everything he had experienced and more, yet she had two children to protect and care for in the process. The inscription read:

Madonna of the Trail. A tribute to pioneers of Arizona and the Southwest, who trod this ground and braved the dangers of the Apache and other warrior tribes. After his encounter with the thieves, Jerry had wished for a dose of civilization. The statue, humbling in its message, came as a clear sign that the town up ahead was exactly that. Bathed in sunshine with its skyline of church spires and trees, and set against a backdrop of mountains thick with Ponderosa pines, there wasn't a town he'd seen that appeared more inviting.

Elms and sycamores and neat clapboard houses lined the side streets. And the first men Jerry spotted were regular-looking, clean-shaven, jeans- and Stetson-wearing cowboys, who touched their brim in recognition of a fellow cowhand riding past.

Highway 60 served as Main Street, and the town was definitely civilized. One of the first things that caught his eye was the marquee of El Rio Theatre: *Now Playing: Jimmy Wakely in Moon Over Montana. Coming Saturday, The Postman Always Rings Twice with Lana Turner and John Garfield.* There were people on the sidewalks pausing to visit with one another. He saw a good many cars parked at the curb in front of Main Street stores, also a few horses hooked to wagons parked there, too. The water tower, "Springerville" painted on its side, loomed above everything at the far end of town. "This reminds me of home, Fan. I like this town."

Jerry stopped first at Becker Mercantile Company on Main Street. They had Denim Riders for $2.98 a pair. He considered buying two, but he already had one extra pair and Fan didn't need to carry more weight than necessary. He did buy a new black Stetson. The day's ride in the sun without a hat had caused his face to feel hot and tender.

Next door at Western Drug Company, a white-coated pharmacist with glasses perched on the end of his nose sold Jerry the Unguentine ointment he needed. A soda fountain covered the length of the drugstore's side wall. In back of the counter were large pictures of milkshakes and cones and banana splits that looked so real it made his mouth water. A slight-built boy, wearing what looked like a paper chef's hat atop his unruly hair, busied himself waiting on customers. Jerry spied the flavor he wanted. "Everything looks delicious. How about a cone with a big scoop of strawberry."

"Yessir, strawberry it is." The boy grabbed a spoon, dipped it in water, and then jammed a scoop of ice cream flecked with strawberries down into a cone. On top of that he piled another mound of ice cream so huge it hung over the sides. "That'll be five cents, sir. Is that big enough for you?"

Jerry handed him a nickel but could only nod and smile, hurriedly licking around the edge to keep it from dripping. He walked outside and sat down on a bench, completely absorbed in eating. Closing his eyes, he was transported back home to the Guthrie kitchen. He was ten years old again and he and his brothers were eating their father's home-made ice cream. He opened his eyes to see Fan staring at him. Suddenly overcome with guilt, Jerry jumped up. "How could I forget you? I know what you like as much as I like ice cream."

Jerry went back into Becker's and while he finished his cone, he bought supplies and a half-dozen apples. When he came out of the store, Fan met him halfway across the sidewalk before he could get to her. She jammed her nose into the bag of apples, expecting *something*. "I know how you feel. Let me cut one up." Jerry popped the last of the cone in his mouth and cut a wedge out of an apple with his pocket knife. Fan's muzzle moved lightly across his palm and the apple wedge disappeared. He cut up two apples for her and put the rest in his saddlebags.

"Another one tomorrow, okay? You deserve some kind of reward for not running off with those mustangs." She smacked and slurped, enjoying her treat as much as Jerry enjoyed his. He wrote a letter to Rolla and Frank while Fan ate. He would write his mother and father when he reached Phoenix. Across the street a barber pole spiraled slowly in its glass cylinder on the front of Troy's Barber Shop. Jerry had promised himself to get a haircut ever since Socorro Police Chief Baca questioned him because of his shaggy appearance. Jerry followed daily grooming habits that were formed by his mother and father long ago and constantly emphasized by Rolla Goodnight. Pride in one's appearance was as ingrained in him as surely as his cowboy skills.

In truth, as much as he wanted a haircut, Jerry wanted to spend time—however short—in the company of men like himself; he wanted to connect again with a familiar world. He led Fan across the street and tied her to a hitching post in front of the barber shop. Inside Lorene's Beauty Shop, next door to Troy's, a pretty blond girl inside smiled at him through the window. Jerry smiled and touched the brim of his hat. *Glad I washed my hair, maybe I don't look as bad as I thought.*

Jerry opened the barber shop door and took in a deep breath. The sharp scent of clean, fragrant shaving soaps and after-shave greeted him. *Lord, that smells good! Why have I never noticed that before?* The polished black and white squares on the floor glistened in the afternoon sun. Two chairs, one of them occupied, filled the small shop. The barber standing behind the empty chair shook out a white drape with a crisp snap. "Name's Troy. Have a seat." Jerry hung his new hat on the rack and closed the door.

"Nice-looking new John B. Get that at Becker's?" Troy fastened the drape around Jerry's neck, ran a comb through his hair, and started snipping.

"I did, so I need a haircut. I'm too shaggy to be wearing such a good-looking Stetson."

"It does look like it's been a while since you had a haircut."

"Eight hundred and fifty miles ago."

"Where's your rig? I see your horse out there."

"She *is* my rig."

The barber's hands paused in mid-air. "You rode eight hundred fifty miles on a horse?" They both looked out at Fan; she was asleep with one rear hoof resting on its edge, her eyes half closed. "How long did that take?" Troy resumed cutting Jerry's hair.

"What's the date today?"

"The first of June."

"Well then, this is my twenty-ninth day."

Troy chuckled. "Amazing. No wonder your horse is napping. Either the law's after you or you got woman trouble."

The other barber nudged his customer. The patron, his face covered by a hot towel, lifted the corner and peeked out at Jerry.

Jerry smiled. "Nah, just making a trip for my grandfather."

"Where you headed on this trip, if you don't mind my asking?"

"Hollywood."

"California?" Troy let out a low whistle. "Virgil. Oliver. Did you hear that? This fella's on his way to Hollywood."

Virgil looked up from his steady slip-slap of the razor against a leather strap. "You mean *the* Hollywood, the one where they make movies?"

Jerry smiled. "That's the one."

"You picked a danged slow way to get there," Troy said.

"Not too slow, I hope. I've got to get there in fifty days to win the bet." With that, the other customer removed the towel from his face and sat up.

"Now that sounds like a story. Hold up, Virgil. I want to hear this." His face glowed pink from the heat, and his voice had an admiring tone.

Troy stopped cutting Jerry's hair. "Oliver's right, you can't say something like that, then leave us hanging. What's the rest of the story?" The three men looked at Jerry expectantly.

"Okay, but you've got to keep cutting. The clock's ticking on that bet and I need to get going." Troy's scissors began snipping again in a fast rhythm. "You ever heard of Charles Goodnight?" Jerry asked.

Troy let out a low whistle. "You bet, pretty much everybody 'round here knows about Charlie Goodnight. The Hashknife Ranch was near here in the old days. It was the biggest spread in the territory, and the story goes that half of Charlie's hands ended up wrangling for Hashknife because he ran them off for drinking or gambling. Hashknife boys were a rowdy bunch, but the head wrangler didn't care."

Virgil spoke up. "But Charlie Goodnight's been dead damned near twenty years. What's he—"

"What about Frank "Pistol Pete" Eaton. Ever hear of him?" Jerry asked.

"Can't say that I have," Virgil said. The others agreed.

"Frank's pretty famous in Oklahoma, Kansas, and Texas. So famous in fact, they copied his mustache and ten gallon hat and made his likeness the mascot of the Oklahoma A & M Cowboys in Stillwater, Oklahoma. *That's* Pistol Pete."

"I'd say that qualifies as being famous," Troy said.

"Frank used to be a gunfighter when he was young, one of Isaac Parker's Deputy Marshals. He's my granddad's best friend and like another grandfather to me. Frank's the one who gave me this six-shooter and the mare to make the ride."

"Is he the one who made the bet?" Oliver said.

"No, my granddad did. With Jimmy Wakely."

"Hold on a minute," Virgil said. "You talking about Jimmy Wakely, the movie star?" Virgil was clearly impressed.

"The very one that's in the movie at El Rio Theater," Jerry said. "That's the first thing I saw when I rode into town."

"This just keeps gettin' better. Gunfighters and movie stars— what's next?" Oliver threw aside his drape and leaned forward in his chair.

The more Jerry talked, the faster Troy's scissors flew; Jerry hoped he was paying attention to what he was doing. "When Jimmy Wakely came to Oklahoma last September to take part in the Cherokee Strip celebration, he told my grandfather that real cowboys are finished. They're soon gonna be a thing of the past. And then he said there isn't a cowboy around worth his salt anymore who could sit in a saddle for the length of a trail drive. That didn't sit well with Grandpa—at all. That's when he bet Jimmy that I could ride from Oklahoma to Holly-wood in fifty days or less. It's about fifteen hundred miles, same as a trail drive."

"Fifteen hundred miles in fifty days. Your grandfather must have a lot of faith in you," Troy said. Virgil and Oliver agreed. "I'm being nosey but I have to ask, how much was this bet?" Troy asked.

"Grandpa would never say how much he bet. I don't know."

"I still don't see what Charlie Goodnight has to do with this," Oliver said.

"My grandpa is Rolla Goodnight, owns the Bar R Ranch outside Enid, Oklahoma. He and Charlie were cousins. Charlie taught him the cattle business. Turned my grandpa into a cowboy, and Grandpa taught me. Well, him and Frank Eaton." Jerry felt a surge of pride.

Troy looked puzzled. "Okay, so your grandfather wins a bet and collects some unknown amount of money from a movie star, but what do you get? Why are you risking your neck?"

The question instantly brought forth the image of the three desperados. "Good question. I guess I wanted to prove Jimmy wrong, wanted to live up to the Goodnight tradition my grandfather believes in so much. When it came right down to it, though, I really wanted to prove to myself I could do it."

Troy removed Jerry's drape and shook it gently, covering the floor beneath the chair with clumps of dark hair. "This haircut is on the house, cowboy. I cut practically every cowboy's hair around Springerville and I'd lay odds that not one of them would ride fifteen hundred miles to win a bet—if he wasn't the one who got the money. I hope you'll let us know when you make it." Troy scribbled his name and address on a piece of paper and handed it to Jerry.

"Thanks, that's mighty nice of you. I will drop you a card. It was a pleasure getting to meet the three of you." Jerry placed the paper in his wallet and put on his new Stetson.

Troy, Virgil, and Oliver each shook his hand and then followed him out of the shop, slapping him on the back and laughing. Across the street three cowboys exited Becker's.

Troy hollered at them. "Come on over here! You gotta meet this fella."

Jerry stood by and listened as his three admirers did the talking. They spilled out his story, interrupting each other, punctuating it with nods and raised eyebrows and a reverent tone when one said "Hollywood" and another said "mooovie star." The cowboys listened attentively and shot Jerry a quick, approving glance when someone mentioned the Goodnight name.

Jerry rode away to a chorus of goodbyes and shouts of good luck. He mailed his letter to Rolla and Frank just before the post office closed for the evening.

"Okay, Fan, we still have a good two or three hours of riding time left."

– 17 –

Geronimo Country

Apache County Independent News, June 1, 1946
• Robson Wins Indy 500 with Record 114.8 MPH •
• Round Valley Mormons Play Host to Top Church Officials •
• Memorial Day Services Include Tribute to
Brothers Gilbert, Malcolm,& Jerold Greer •

Jerry looked back over his shoulder at the El Rio Theatre neon sign flashing pink, green, and white. "Places like that offset the bad times, don't they, Fan." Her ears flicked back and forth, but otherwise Fan gave no response. "It would be nice if you could talk. This trip would be a lot more interesting." The thought of Fan talking made Jerry smile. After some of their adventures, it was very likely he might not want to hear what she had to say at all.

"I've proved something. So have you, girl, even if it's to nobody but you and me." Jerry's smile deepened. The image of the discharged, crippled-up seaman-student full of doubts about himself had vanished along with the fears about his back. The anguish and fear, so real only a few months ago, now seemed like a long-ago bad dream.

Everywhere he looked Jerry saw lush pastures filled with Herefords; other enclosures held sheep. Troy had mentioned that John Wayne owned a ranch around Springerville, a tantalizing thought that they might be riding over his property. It stirred images of gunslingers and range wars between cattlemen and sheep men. "You're riding over famous ground, Fan. Some of the biggest gunfighters in the territory used to hang out here. The Clanton gang, all hundred of them lived somewhere around here. Byron knows all about Ike and the other two Clantons shooting it out with Wyatt Earp and Doc Holiday at the OK Corral. And Butch Cassidy and Billy the Kid did their carousing in town, at different times, of course. It's too bad Byron couldn't have come. He would love it here—probably never get him to leave." Fan gave no acknowledgment. Jerry applied a little pressure with his knees and Fan snorted. "That's better."

Jerry dropped south of the highway and rode alongside the White River through alpine meadows blanketed with wild yellow daisies. He passed waterfalls that spilled into the river over volcanic rock thick with brush and outlined in ferns.

He fished for his supper; a big Cutthroat practically jumped into his skillet. "Look at that!" Jerry held up the fish in Fan's direction. "If Grandpa and Frank knew they could put a pole in the water and catch a twelve-inch trout in five minutes, they would never want to leave this place either." Fan, busy grazing on the thick grass, did not look his way. Jerry whistled and she raised her head, ears alertly forward. Fan walked over to him. "Atta, girl. If for some reason, we ever got separated, I need to be able to count on you." Jerry rewarded her with an apple.

Few signs of man existed to interrupt the tranquility. Jerry spotted white tail deer, free-roaming elk, and pronghorn antelope herds. One morning he caught a glimpse of a distant brown bear with her two cubs. No matter the direction that Jerry gazed, he saw dramatic landscapes. Majestic peaks carpeted with pines, firs, and spruce loomed high on both sides. At the base of the mountains stood thick stands of aspens, their white trunks and pale shimmering leaves contrasting sharply against the dark ponderosas and silvery blue-green spruce.

It wasn't until they passed the Fort Apache Timber Company the following day that he realized they were on reservation land. The whine of machines filled the stillness, and Jerry breathed in the acrid smell of processing lumber instead of cool pine-scented air. They reached the Mogollon Rim at mid-day. Jerry removed Fan's saddle and she immediately rolled in the dirt. "You love that. Why is that? You like the way it scratches your skin or do you just like getting dirty?" He watered and fed her and Fan slept while he fixed his lunch. Jerry ate his meal, all the while looking out over yet another incredible vista.

The Mogollon Rim, the geographical shelf where the Colorado Plateau ended, towered three thousand feet above the southwest desert. He looked out over hills and rocks, cliffs, canyons, and mesas—an earthen maze of red and gold and every shade of brown. Phoenix waited for them somewhere in the distance—the desert. Thoughts of *the desert* conjured up visions of searing heat, unquenchable thirst, and endless sand. At a gut level, it stirred the same fear as Jerry's first glimpse of the Texas panhandle and the Rockies. But his concern proved to be unfounded.

Thankfully, the temperature of this eastern Arizona desert was warm, not hot, and Jerry found plenty of full creeks. He reminded himself that the land around him had once been home to Geronimo and, like the history of the Llano Estacado, the image of the Apache Chief made him ride taller in the saddle.

Once they were out of the canyons, Jerry held the reins loosely and Fan settled into her jog and lope gait. They passed Apache dwellings, eight-sided mud and log hogans, each one with a garden close by. Also beside each hogan was a large area planted in corn, lush and green and about ankle high. Some had horses tethered in front, and it seemed that every hogan had children playing outside. At one, a woman sat cross-legged on a mat near the blanket-covered opening. Her hands flew back and forth across a loom, the rhythm of their movement interrupted occasionally to push a wooden cradle. She glanced up at rider and horse but quickly looked back at her work. Jerry rode past buckboards and horse-drawn wagons packed with young and elder Indian family members. He passed groups of Apache men and boys riding bareback. Some dressed like white men. Others, especially the younger ones, wore no shirt, only leather vests over their bare chests with long leather pants fringed down the side. All of them had long black hair, either flowing loosely or tied into a braid. And none of them gave Jerry more than a curious glance.

At Cibecue, an Apache trading post village, Jerry got to see where everyone was headed; an all-Indian rodeo had just started when he rode in. Four more hours of daylight remained, but he couldn't let Fan ride any farther. They had covered thirty-five miles since early morning, half of which had been in the high country. She needed rest.

The Cibecue Trading Post seemed to be headquarters for the rodeo activities. Horses stood side-by-side, tethered to the rail in front. Some resembled Fan in color and markings except that none of them had saddles. Strewn across the dirt field in front of the trading post were horse-drawn wagons and buckboards of every description and parked every which way. Jerry found a shady place and picketed Fan to a hitching rail nailed to a tree a short distance away. While he questioned whether he should let her drink from the nearby watering trough, Fan plunged her muzzle in the water and began drinking before he could dismount.

Jerry looked around for other white people but found none. It struck him as odd that the Apaches gave him nothing more than a passing glance; he gratefully moved among them unacknowledged. He walked among old men deep in conversation, their bronzed faces etched with lines. They looked ancient and full of wisdom; they spoke with a cadence and guttural softness that made their words sound musical, though unintelligible to Jerry. Out of the corner of his eye, he watched an elder remove his hat to wipe his brow. He wore his gray hair braided in two long braids and coiled into a perfect circle on top of his head. After he had wiped his brow with his sleeve, the elder placed the hat back on top to hold the coil in place. Jerry smiled, silently reminding himself to tease Frank that he'd found him a new hairdo for his braids.

Jerry walked close to short, brown grandmothers with silvery hair and missing teeth, young mothers with papooses strapped to their backs, and lean young men strutting like roosters in front of smiling girls. The women wore long velvet skirts decorated with silver beads and conch shells. Calf-length moccasins peeked from under their skirts as they walked and moved. All wore their hair in braids and, except for a few very young girls, all the women were plump. Some of the children spoke English to a playmate and received a reply back in Apache. They scooted around and by Jerry, laughing and shouting, raising clouds of red dust as they chased each other and their skinny, yapping dogs.

Jerry walked up to a large arena surrounded by onlookers and rested his arms on the fence. Inside the enclosure, a bronc rider, still attached to his bareback mount, whooped and hollered as the wild-eyed sorrel tried to dislodge him.

Nearby, two rows of make-shift tents sold food, filling the air with smoke and some of the best smells Jerry had ever inhaled. Following one pungent sweet aroma to its source, he bought hot Indian fry bread. He ate beef and wild game cooked over open flame, and ears of multicolored corn just plucked from boiling water: the corn was sweet and finger-burning hot. One woman sold roasted pinion nuts. He observed another woman selling hot tortillas made from corn he saw her grind on a *metate,* pat into rounds, then fry over a fire in front of her tent.

Women were in charge of selling the food. Jerry held out his palm covered with coins and nodded for them to take what they wanted for the food. Pudgy fingers moved across his palm like Fan's muzzle collecting an apple wedge. They picked out a nickel for the bread or two pennies for an ear of corn. Jerry saw no liquor, but everywhere stacked in the shade, he saw wooden crates filled with bottles of orange, grape, and raspberry soda pop. And it seemed that every man, woman, and child had one in his or her hand. He stayed until twilight, watching Brahma and longhorn bull-riding, calf-roping, and bronc-riding events.

When later he made camp alongside Cibecue Creek, south of the trading post, Jerry ate more Indian fry bread, more meat and more ears of corn, until he felt stuffed. After Fan drank her fill and ate a large portion of grain, she polished off the corn cobs Jerry saved for her. It had been a special day, getting to be among the Apache people in their world. Jerry desperately wanted to remember this day: young people flirting, ancient men trading stories, and bright-eyed grandchildren clinging to skirts while their grandmothers cooked and laughed— sharing something that would forever be unknown to a white man. This was a rare gift, getting to peel aside a curtain and glimpse into a culture as ancient as this land they called home.

Again, Jerry silently thanked his grandfather for making the bet.

He lit a match and quickly rechecked his map. The Salt River Canyon lay sixteen miles ahead, directly in their path to Phoenix. Several forks of the White River, the Black River, and farther west the Canyon, Cibecue, and Carrizo Creeks flowed into the Salt River. It looked to be of a pretty good size and it ran right through the canyon they had to cross.

"Water ahead, Fan. Bath time, laundry time. You love water; you're going to love this."

– 18 –

The Letter

The Guthrie Daily Leader, June 8, 1946
• *World Food Crisis Prompts War Dept Study of Farmers' Early Discharge* •
• *Japan's Tojo Pleads Innocent Before International Tribunal to
Charges of Aggression, Plunder, War* •

Rolla Goodnight exited Taylor's Trading Company, his arms loaded with groceries. He headed toward his truck parked on Main Street near the blacksmith shop where he dropped Frank off. As Rolla passed Marshall, Oklahoma's post office, the post mistress burst out the door, obviously excited. She had an envelope in her hand. "Oh, Mr. Goodnight, I'm glad I saw you. This letter just arrived and it's addressed to you." She rushed forward. "It looks to be from Jerry— from Arizonaah."

"Well, thanks for flaggin' me down, I appreciate it. Could you drop it in my grocery bag?" Rolla walked a few more steps then put the bags down and extracted the letter. He held it at arm's length, trying to make out the postmark when he heard a voice behind him. He turned around. It was Carlton Scheir, a high school friend of Jerry's. "What are you up to, Carlton?"

"On the way to my new job," Carlton said. "Mister and Missus Taylor hired me to stock shelves. Have you heard from Jerry?"

"Got his first letter right here. We had a postcard from New Mexico. He said Fan had a go-round with distemper. I'm anxious to hear what he says." Rolla put on his glasses. "This one's from Springerville, Arizona, so his horse must have come out okay."

111

"That sure is something, Jerry riding all the way to California. I'd be afraid of doing something like that."

"Afraid, a young fellow like you? Why, you can do anything you set your mind to."

Carlton shook his head. "You sound like my dad, but when he says it, he's just talking about me going to Phillips University and majoring in business, not riding a horse half way across the country."

"Why, cowboys been doing what Jerry's doing since before I was born. Wish I coulda gone with him. I haven't ridden through that part of the country since I helped Charlie Goodnight take some herds through sixty years ago."

"I heard you made some kind of a bet with Jimmy Wakely. If anybody can win it, Jerry can. If he calls, please be sure to tell him everyone round here is rooting for him, especially me."

"I'll make it a point to pass that along to his mama. He'll be calling her."

"Goodbye, sir. Tell Mr. Eaton hello for me."

The hot sun beat down as Rolla greeted several other Marshall residents. He shuffled grocery bags from one arm to the other each time someone stopped him. One neighbor in bib overalls, his wife in a wash dress, stopped to ask about Jerry. Another neighbor came up, tipped his hat and then joined the conversation. Before he reached his truck, Rolla was greeted by three or four more people, all of them asking about Jerry. Every person, man and woman, said how proud Rolla and his whole family must be of Jerry doing such a fine, brave thing.

Rolla mulled over his neighbors' comments about Jerry, all the way back to his truck parked in the shade of the town's water tower. A rickety structure, *Marshall* had long ago been painted on the tower in red, but was now faded to almost unreadable.

Rolla put his groceries inside the truck and puzzled over the fact that most of the people who stopped him were twenty or thirty years younger than he, some more than that. Yet all of them acted like

Jerry's ride was the next most dangerous thing to fighting on Iwo Jima. It was disturbing to Rolla, an unexpected attitude that made him feel uncertain. Could it be that Jimmy was right that the ride they sent Jerry on couldn't be done? Rolla spotted Frank, holster around his hips, saying goodbye to the blacksmith as he exited his shop. He climbed into the truck.

"Everybody in Marshall knows about the bet, Frank. Is there anybody in town you missed tellin'?" Rolla said as he started the truck.

"Nosiree, I think I pretty much told everybody. What's got you all riled up? You look like somebody fed you skunk soup."

"Tell me somethin'. How many times did you make a ride like Jerry's?"

"You talkin' me, by myself?"

"Yup." Rolla shifted into first gear and steered the Chevy onto Main Street.

"Half a dozen, prob'ly. Countin' the drives you 'n me did, another dozen."

"I just had ten people tell me what a brave thing Jerry's doing. I talked to Jerry's friend, Carlton Schier, same age as Jerry. He said he'd be too afraid to do that. The postmistress gave me a letter from Jerry and, the way she acted, you'd think it was from the President. I'm thinkin' I think a lot different than these other folks. What do you think?"

"Soon as I figure out your question, I'll answer." Frank, silent for a moment, waved as they passed a barefooted youngster. "Maybe you need a dose of castor oil." He chuckled.

"You know damn well what I mean," Rolla groused.

"Well, nobody thought it was especially brave in our day. Us cowboys did it for a livin', but I guess it ain't so common anymore so people are gonna look at it different."

Rolla handed Frank the envelope. "Here's Jerry's letter."

"Well, glory be, how 'bout I read it while you drive? You look mighty anxious."

"I ain't worried-anxious. I'm…curious-anxious."

"Wait a minute. I need my spectacles." Frank fished wire-rimmed glasses out of his shirt pocket and stretched them behind each ear, one earpiece at a time. He adjusted the envelope to various lengths from his eyes.

"How 'bout doing it today? We only got five miles to go."

"You get that hitch outta your getalong." Frank carefully slit the envelope with his pocket knife and withdrew the letter. *Dear Grandpa and Frank.* "Why ain't that nice, he made it to me too."

"Well o'course he made it to you, too. Will you get on it with it, or do I have to pull this truck over and take that letter away from you, you ornery old cuss?"

Frank cleared his throat and continued to read. *"I'm sitting here having an ice cream cone in Springerville, Arizona. It's a nice town after some I've seen. I'm eating pretty good, especially over the Rockies. I had me about every kind of small game there is (thanks, Grandpa). Still, I'm sick of beans. This is the first ice cream I've had on the trip and does it ever taste good. I sure miss Mama's peach cobbler and your biscuits and ham gravy.*

I'm a little better than half way to Hollywood. This is surely the hard way to get there, just ask Fan. Ha Ha. She is doing fine now, but thinner I can tell. I've seen some beautiful country. Will be able to tell some trail stories of my own when I get back. Everything you taught me came in handy when I got jumped by three mean-looking Mexicans on the Continental Divide. They meant to kill me and take everything I had. One guy drew on me so I had no choice but outdraw him (thanks, Frank). The last thing I remember saying before I pulled the trigger was, 'fill your hand you SOB.' I didn't even realize I said it, it just popped out. I winged the guy and the three of them took off.

"Well, I'll be dawg!" Frank howled with laughter and slapped his knee.

Rolla hit the steering wheel with the heel of his hand. "Damn them crooks, if that don't beat all, I didn't figure on something like that happenin'. Go ahead, what else does he say?"

"Grandpa, you'll be happy to know that so far, a lot of what I've seen doesn't look like it's changed. The Palo Duro looked exactly like you described it. The Llano Estacado west of Clovis, must look the same as when you rode through. And Frank, I'm pretty sure Ft. Sumner didn't look much different when your friend Pat Garrett shot the Kid. Did you get the book? Speaking of Billy, for a day or two I felt like Jerry the Kid. Ha Ha. I'm real glad I made the trip and grateful to be on schedule. Lots of things have happened, but I handled them, like you said. I may come out of this a cowboy yet. Thanks to both of you for all you taught me. Your loving grandson and friend, Jerry

Rolla stared straight ahead, an uneasy feeling gripping him. "I never give it a thought that somebody would try to kill Jerry. You think he'll be all right?"

Frank was re-reading the letter and chuckling. "Fill your hand, you sonofa...exactly like I taught him. Quit your worryin', Rolla. Nothin's gonna get the best of Jerry Van Meter. That man's gonna be fine."

– 19 –

A River Ran Over Us

Fort Apache Reservation News, June 4, 1946
• *Antelope Herd Increase Noted* •
• *Wild Dog Control Ordered by Tribal Council* •
• *Fort Apache 4-H Club Hosts 275 Navajo Members* •

The sixteen miles to the Salt River Canyon turned out to be hard miles. They rode up one hill and down another then up yet another, all the while descending in elevation. Jerry and Fan wound their way through sun-heated arroyos and canyons, Jerry using his compass to navigate through the maze-like landscape. He wanted to get across the river, have lunch, and then rest Fan on the other side.

They reached the canyon rim and Jerry began looking for a trail down to the river. Mesquite, sage, and brittlebush thrived in the rock-strewn earth and made finding the entrance difficult. When he did find it, the path was narrow, steep, rocky, and well-worn. The trail hugged the mountain side of the steep canyon for thirty feet down, ending on a flattened-out ridge. The elongated ledge obscured any view of the bottom of the canyon and the river. But, if his map was correct, the trail picked up again somewhere along the ridge, for it clearly showed that it led all the way to the canyon floor.

They had descended ten feet down the path when Fan's leg brushed against a mesquite bush, but by the time Jerry saw the rattler coiled in the shade, it had already struck at Fan. She shied; her hooves slipped on the decomposed rock, and both of them went over the trail edge. Jerry had no time to dive off. With his left leg pinned beneath

Fan's flank, together they slid twenty feet down the steep embankment to the flattened-out ridge below.

When the noise of falling rocks stopped, the only sound interrupting the stillness was their breathing. Fan lay perfectly still as though gauging whether she was hurt. Finally, she struggled to her feet. During the fall Jerry had let go of the reins; nothing held her now. "Come on, Fan. Here, girl," Jerry said from the ground. He tried to keep his voice calm, not sure she was okay, and worried that if she was, she would bolt and run.

Jerry suddenly became aware of his leg, one long bloody scratch that felt like it was on fire. The left leg of his jeans from mid-thigh down to his boot no longer existed; a few small shreds remained, attached only by the inside seam. Struggling to his feet, Jerry put his full weight on it. "Thank God, it's not broken," he whispered in relief.

Jerry stepped forward and reached for the reins. Fan backed up. "Come on, girl, don't do this," he said softly. "We're in the middle of nowhere." Fan tossed her head and snorted. He spoke in as soothing a voice as he could muster. "Remember outside Springerville when I said we might get separated and I needed to be able to count on you?" Fan pawed the ground. *She's ready to take off.* Jerry held his outstretched hand steady and whistled an easy whistle. "This is one of those times. Can I count on you, Fan?" He held his breath and waited. Fan seemed to think it over, then ambled toward him and nuzzled his outstretched hand. Jerry exhaled a sigh of relief. "You are one great horse, girl. The best."

Jerry gathered her reins and stroked her neck. "Good girl, Fan." He ran his hands down her trembling legs. "No broken bones, no snake bite. Your flank doesn't even have a mark on it." Jerry instantly realized how his leg got so badly scratched. It had held Fan away from the rocky embankment during the slide. He fished an apple out of the saddle bag. "This is for being able to count on you. You earned this."

A sure-footed horse, Fan's fall was bad luck, pure and simple. Jerry dismissed it and tried to ignore his stinging leg. Grateful that they hadn't rolled down the embankment, that his leg hadn't been crushed, and that Fan came out of the slide uninjured, Jerry said a silent thank you and mounted up. Finding the continuation of the trail, he resumed their descent, this time avoiding bushes. The lower part of the trail was four times longer. Jerry kept a close eye on the path and let Fan pick her way. If they went over the edge here it wouldn't matter about the bet or Hollywood, or anything else.

Jerry's leg was bleeding, the skin embedded with sand and rocks, throbbing now and stinging even worse. The river would clean away the dirt. As soon as they crossed, Jerry would put Bag Balm on it. A soothing ointment that no cowboy was ever without, Bag Balm helped cure horses' scrapes and scratches; it would help his raw leg as well.

Jerry heard the river before he saw it. When he rode up to its edge, the roar drowned out all other sound. Greater across than the length of a football field, the river almost filled the canyon. The walls on the other side of the river consisted of two tiers of almost vertical walls, each tier hundreds of feet high. Jerry could only stare and try to fight his rising panic. *There's no place to get out of the river if we do make it across. This couldn't be any more dangerous.*

He didn't see a ridge or water line, which told Jerry the river was at its highest level. High water and a fast current had ripped out trees on its journey through the canyon, toppling them into the river and gathering debris in their branches. Directly in front of them and half-way across, the river was split into two raging torrents by an island of massive boulders. The current thundered around and over the boulders then plunged twenty feet, producing a deafening roar and kicking up spray fifty feet into the air. It was a breathtaking sight but an impossible place to cross. Jerry rode for thirty minutes up and down the narrow bank, trying to find a flat expanse of river where boulders and waterfalls were two less things to worry about. Spotting a few shallow beaches on the other side, he realized their only chance would be to aim for one of those. Dismounting, Jerry's heart pounded as Fan waded into the water and started drinking.

"Hang on a minute, will you?" He put his six-shooter in the tin with his calendar and writing pad, tied the saddlebags up on top, and secured the Winchester on top of it all. He hoped it would keep everything out of the water. Jerry looked straight up at the cliff above him. *We can't go back. We'd never make it to Hollywood on time.* He thought about removing his boots and adding them to the pile, but the river bottom looked to be as rocky as the shore. He decided against it.

Jerry patted Fan's neck and shouted. "I know you love water, but I never figured on anything like this. Let's stick together, okay?" He knew she couldn't hear him above the roar but it didn't matter, this was going to be a roll of the dice. Fan moved into the current and Jerry followed, panic and excitement taking over as icy water poured into his boots. "I hate cold water," he shouted at the river. Jerry jammed his hat firmly on his head and took hold of Fan's tail. "Okay, Fan, let's swim this damn river."

No sooner had the words left his mouth than the riverbed beneath Jerry's feet disappeared. He felt Fan's body float free and her powerful rear legs displace the water beneath him. Jerry forced himself to breathe evenly and paddle with strong, even strokes with his right hand. He held tight to Fan's tail with his left. Never had they crossed a river this wide or wild while training in Oklahoma. Never had they been swept downstream faster than their forward progress. Jerry felt Fan's power pulling them and he paddled and kicked, trying to keep his focus on the far bank. The blur of canyon walls on the opposite side looked closer; they were making progress.

Jerry and Fan reached mid-river. Without warning, a strong circular current enveloped them, spinning Fan and Jerry around in a circle, dizzying and disorienting. When they stopped turning, it took a minute for Jerry to get his bearings. They had turned counter-clockwise several times; Fan's head now pointed down river. The current slammed him up against her right flank and he could feel her struggling. Fan's front leg brushed dangerously close to his and Jerry pushed away to get out of the way of her powerful hooves. "C'mon, swim!" Jerry shouted.

He had no idea if Fan heard him. A diagonal wave—a surge of water—swamped Jerry and he went under. No calm, steady, even strokes now. He fought to reach the surface, kicking and paddling with all his strength. Another surge lifted his Stetson and Jerry instinctively let go of Fan's tail and grabbed it. "NO," he screamed when he realized what he'd done.

His voice was lost in the river's roar.

Without Fan's massive weight holding him, Jerry floated free, racing down the river, bobbing under and out of the water like a piece of wood. He looked back; Fan's head, a small dot, showed above the surface of the choppy water, then he couldn't see her at all. Because of his water-filled boots, Jerry raced down the river nearly vertical in the water, fighting with everything he had to keep his head up, not completely successful. Each time he surfaced, he tried to dodge boulders and free-floating logs. Battling the water's force, Jerry watched canyon walls race by at frightening speed; he had to try harder. He took a deep breath, clamped the brim of his Stetson between his teeth, and started kicking and pulling through the water. Jaws clenched on the Stetson's brim, refusing to give up a second hat on this trip.

The canyon curved, its walls now closer together compressing the river's flow. Jerry felt the water rise like a bucking bronco, roaring higher and faster. With the opposite bank closer, he battled with renewed energy. Up ahead and coming up fast, he caught sight of a dead tree angled into the water—a chance! The icy waters had numbed his arms and legs; Jerry hoped they would cooperate. With a burst of energy, he pulled himself in line with the tree. It was coming right at his face.

He had a split-second to stick his arms out in front and kick hard to raise his head. Jerry hit the tree square-on with the upper part of his chest. He wrapped his arms around it, closed his eyes and hung on with all his might. How long he remained that way he had no idea, but when he opened his eyes he was ten feet away from the bank. It took him a concentrated effort to unclench his jaws. Only when he felt sharp pain in his jaws and both sides of his neck, did he believe he had succeeded. Jerry released his Stetson, jammed it on his head, and began making his way toward shore. The river's force kept him jammed against the tree trunk; he had to inch his way along, rough bark and broken branches ripping his shirt, scratching his chest and arms; he felt nothing.

Then there it was—ground beneath his feet. Beautiful, solid, dammitall Mother Earth. Jerry crawled out of the water and collapsed on the bank.

– 20 –

Hon-dah, Se-eh-ha, **Brother**

Fort Apache Reservation News, June 4, 1946
• *Council to Study Proposed Indian Medical Center* •
• *5 Boys, 8 Girls Born at Whiteriver Health Service Hospital* •
• *Tribal Fair Queen to be Chosen in August* •

The mud felt soft and comforting, as warm as the river was cold. Jerry lay unmoving and fought to keep from passing out. It took what seemed like an interminable time for any feeling to return to his arms and legs but when it did, it was accompanied with the sting and pain of his cuts and abrasions. Every limb ached from the strain and his arms and legs felt as though they each weighed a hundred pounds.

Jerry rolled over and sat up; he looked around trying to get his bearings. In front of him the pinion tree that saved his life remained horizontal in the water, the river roaring over it determined to remove anything that stood in its way. Had the current claimed Fan? Had she gotten out? And if she did, where? Torn between hope and panic, Jerry told himself that he'd rather she drowned than be lying on the bank badly injured. The thought of having to put Fan down filled him with gut-wrenching despair. Tears welled; Jerry's heart sank.

Every movement took effort; he finally got his heavy boots off and poured the water out. The thought occurred that his boots may very well have saved his life, their weight keeping him vertical in the river's wild ride. He said a silent thanks that he hadn't tied them to Fan's saddle. Jerry struggled to his feet and stood for a moment, waiting for his trembling legs to regain their strength. He glanced at

123

his surroundings; fortunately he had landed on a long stretch of narrow beach that ran alongside the base of the cliffs. Back across the river, sheer canyon walls rose hundreds of feet straight up from the water's edge—no beach, no chance of escape. *I'm either damned lucky or blessed*, he thought as he started to walk.

Jerry had no idea how long he had been in the water. His watch was in the tin on Fan's saddle—*wherever that might be*. The sun beat straight down; it was about noon, he thought. Jerry kept walking, expecting at any moment to run out of beach. It continued so narrow at times that his boots filled with water, and two or three times the beach disappeared altogether. He then had to scramble over boulders or hang onto bushes until he found another stretch of sand.

Jerry kept his eyes on the sand, searching for any clue that Fan had made it out of the river, but so far—nothing. Everything looked familiar. With each step came a sinking feeling, and finally panic. He felt dizzy and disoriented. Could he already have passed the spot where they entered the river? Jerry started to run. The bank curved, the beach widened, and there they were—Fan's hoof prints leading out of the river. "She made it!" he shouted above the river's roar, his voice bouncing off the canyon walls.

Jerry dropped to his knees and examined the prints, which gave no evidence of a limp or injury. Their depth in the sand told Jerry she stood there for a while. "You waited for me. Where are you, Fan?" He looked around. Alone and scared, she could be anywhere. Jerry struggled to his feet and followed her hoof prints to the base of the canyon wall. Fan had found a trail! Her prints disappeared a few feet up the steep path. Exhausted, cut and bleeding, without food or the means to get it, Jerry fully appreciated his predicament. He stood for a moment to gather strength, his only thought that Fan made it out alive provided adrenalin and hope. A path leading up from the river, they still had a chance. *Fan took this path and I am going to find her.*

Not wanting to spoil his momentary good feeling, Jerry dreaded looking up. When he did, he sucked in his breath. The cliff walls rose so high they disappeared—eight hundred feet at least if they were the same height as the cliffs on the other side of the river. A glance back across at the sheer vertical walls confirmed his estimate; he exhaled a sigh of resignation. No doubt just as high and equally tough, but it was his only way out of this canyon—and the river.

The blistering sun beat down, radiating heat off the rocks on both sides of him, heating the air he breathed. Jerry scrambled and half-crawled up the narrow trail, every few minutes stopping to catch his breath and let his heartbeat slow. He refused to think about rattle snakes, about muscles screaming from exertion, how thirsty he was, or how much his injured leg hurt. The river had washed away dirt and gravel, but his wound was bleeding again. He fantasized that Fan would be waiting for him at the top. *Just keep putting one foot in front of the other.*

Jerry didn't know how many hours it took, but it had to be late afternoon when he heaved himself up the last step of the trail onto flat ground. He tried to straighten up but couldn't. Gasping for air and still grunting from the exertion, he remained bent over, eyes closed, hands on his thighs. When at last he could stand straight, he looked around; there was no pinto mare waiting for him. Instead, he saw half the state of Arizona stretched out before him.

The sun's position told Jerry it was about four o'clock and he was looking in a westerly direction. To his right were terraces and tiers of jagged cliffs that led up to higher barren-looking slopes. Straight ahead was a broad alluvial plain, an occasional tree or two interrupting the horizon and providing depth—visible markers of the magnitude of the landscape.

He squinted at the skyline, for a moment thinking it was a mirage, until he blinked and squinted harder—no mirage. In the distance under some trees, he made out the figures of two men and three horses! Jerry instinctively headed toward them. "God, I pray that one of those horses is Fan and whoever those men are, they're friendly."

Jerry's mind swirled with possibilities. He had thoroughly studied his map the evening he left Cibecue and in the process discovered an interesting feature: the Lost Dutchman mine was nearby. Supposedly the mountain was full of hidden gold, and legend had it that the dream of every unhinged tourist and adventurous Arizonan was to find it. Recalling that made him wonder about the men; were they prospectors or gun-toting treasure hunters? Hopefully they weren't thieves like the ones in Quemado. With one leg of his jeans gone and his leg bleeding, would they think that he was a crazy prospector himself? Only about half of his shirt had survived, its remnants unable to hide the cuts and scratches from the tree that saved his life.

A lone figure on foot, with an empty holster and everything he owned on Fan, Jerry fought down panic as he approached. As he drew closer he recognized the two men were young Apache braves. Their horses were tethered to a paloverde tree. And the most wonderful sight since spotting Fan's hoof prints in the sand—was Fan herself! Jerry wiped away instant tears with his hand when Fan looked up him and nickered. Even more wonderful, she looked fine!

Camped in the shade of the trees, the braves' dwindling fire and empty spit told him they had been there for a while. Dressed like the young men he had seen on the way to Cibecue, they wore fringed leather pants, with vests over their bare chests. One of them had pulled his long black hair straight back in a pony tail and tied it with leather; the other parted his hair in the middle and had two long braids that hung down his back. They were both gnawing on a leg of game that looked like jackrabbit. Jerry's empty stomach wrenched tighter at the sight and aroma of food. He spotted his Winchester on the ground between them, next to Fan's saddle. She looked unconcerned, happy even. Standing in the shade next to the other horses, she was nibbling at the withers of a handsome Appaloosa.

Jerry realized he didn't have a prayer if he had to fight. Like crossing the Salt River, this was another roll of the dice, a crap shoot. He took a deep breath, attempted a smile, and stopped on the opposite side of their fire. Standing as steady as his wobbly legs would allow, he raised his right hand in a gesture he hoped looked friendly. He greeted them. "I come from the land of *Tsa-La-Gi*—the Cherokee."

Black eyes set in bronzed implacable faces stared back at him. They said nothing. *They must not speak English.* Jerry tried again. He made a fist and touched his heart, then pointed at Fan. "Thank you for finding horse. I...me...very happy."

The Apache with the braids tossed aside the sucked-clean bone and looked at his friend. They spoke a few words. The second Apache chuckled and said something back. Both men stood up at the same time. Jerry straightened, his eyes searching their faces for a clue what they were going to do.

The Apache brave with the ponytail spoke. "*Hon-dah, se-eh-ha.* That is 'welcome, elder brother' in our language. Your English is very bad for a white man." His greeting did not include a smile, but his voice held no threat and echoed the soft guttural cadence Jerry had heard at Cibecue. Standing on the other side of the fire, Jerry experienced a glimmer of hope.

Two Braids gestured at the landscape. "You are lucky we find your mare. She would soon be buzzard meat out here."

The realization they meant him no harm, combined with hunger, the heat and his exhaustion, took away whatever it was that held Jerry upright. Drained of all energy, he sagged to his knees and then collapsed down on the ground, his legs out in front of him. "I'm the one who would be buzzard bait. That was a helluva walk up the trail from the river." He spoke in a dry raspy whisper; he felt dizzy and lightheaded.

"You look bad, like you lost more than the mare. You have a fight?" Pony Tail asked.

"Yeah, with the river and it almost won. That's how we got separated." Jerry nodded toward Fan. He gingerly touched his leg. "This happened when we slid down the top part of the trail on the other side of the canyon."

"River running full now, not good time to cross," Two Braids said. "Your leg looks bad. You need medicine."

"I looked for a better place, but couldn't find one. Me 'n my horse have come too far to turn around now. Fan and I started out in Oklahoma. We're on our way to Hollywood."

The men spoke rapidly to each other and then Two Braids addressed Jerry. "I am known as William." The one with the ponytail told Jerry he could call him Elias. "We see movies sometimes at Theodore Roosevelt School in Cibecue. You a movie star?" Elias asked.

"No star, just a cowboy. My name is Jerry Van Meter and I got to see a little of the Cibecue rodeo. I'm surprised you didn't see me. I kinda stuck out like a sore thumb."

William shook his head. "Didn't have time to look around, too busy trying to hang on to a Brahma. He didn't much like Apaches." He motioned in Elias' direction. "Elias did better bronc riding."

Jerry had ridden bulls and broncs in half a dozen rodeos in high school around Enid and Guthrie. When he told them how his first bronc had sent him airborne, William and Elias smiled for the first time. They offered Jerry the rest of their rabbit and water. Between bites, Jerry told them about the trip, about Fan getting distemper, and the snowstorm he had encountered.

"No wonder you look bad. We are on our way to Cibecue," Elias said. "You come with us. We take you to our medicine man. His herbs can fix your leg. You buy new clothes at trading post—cheap," William added, eyeing Jerry's tattered jeans. "We have to cross river, but we know a place not so dangerous."

Jerry grinned and shook his head. "Thank you for the offer, but I've got some stuff to put on my leg. And I'm exhausted; I don't think I could make it across that river again even with you two carrying me." They nodded that they understood.

Jerry finished his food and struggled to his feet. William untied Fan, brought her forward and waited as Elias saddled her. William then retrieved Jerry's Winchester and shoved it in the scabbard attached to the saddle. "Fine rifle," he said. "You will need it. Game is good around here, plenty of jack rabbits, javelinas, too." Elias handed Fan's reins to Jerry.

Grateful and happy that she looked unhurt, Jerry wanted to throw his arms around her neck. Instead he stroked her flank. He eyed the two men, his hand still on Fan. "Thank you, William. You, too, Elias. I will always remember what you did. You saved my life."

"If you make movie in Hollywood, make sure this time Indians win," William said and shot a quick grin at Elias. "We don't like John Wayne movies. Indians are always bad. They scare even us."

Jerry couldn't suppress a chuckle. Rolla had insisted that he carry silver dollars—for emergencies, he said. The Salt River certainly qualifies, he thought. He handed a coin to each of them.

"Is not necessary you pay. We—"

"This is a gift from a friend, not pay. Please. I want you to have them."

"Our custom is if you give gift, we must give also and we have nothing," Elias said. William nodded.

"You gave me back my horse and all my things. You shared your meal. Those are big gifts. My gift is much smaller." William and Elias looked at each other and back at Jerry, then nodded their acceptance. Jerry fished out his writing pad and wrote down their names, in care of the Cibecue Trading Post, Fort Apache Indian Reservation, Arizona. They said they would like a picture "from movie land." Jerry thanked them again and said he would mail them a picture, then mounted up and headed Fan toward Phoenix.

In his first few minutes in the saddle Jerry became painfully aware of every muscle in his body. He ached from exhaustion and the strain of the eight hundred foot climb. He hurt from being battered by the river. He felt something else even more acutely; an awareness of the hundred different things that could have happened, the majority of them bad. That they both survived without serious injury, that he had

Fan back and they were once again on their way seemed no small miracle.

"Thank you, Lord. This can only be Your doing. Yours and two very fine Apaches."

The Salt Canyon and the river crossing had cost Jerry more than a shirt, a pair of jeans, and a couple of silver dollars. It cost precious time on a journey that had none to spare.

Three days' ride from Phoenix, somewhere in the Superstition Mountains, the thought that he might not make it to Hollywood in time crossed Jerry's mind for the first time.

– 21 –

The Mountain Lion

The Arizona Republic, June 5, 1946
• *Phoenix War Plants Convert, Provide Peacetime Employment* •
• *Prisoner of War Club Hopes to Reach State's 250 Ex-Prisoners* •
• *Bullet Bob Feller Pitches 10th Victory for Cleveland* •

Late the next afternoon, Jerry and Fan reached the base of Rockinstraw Mountain, its formidable terrain covered with huge boulders, cacti, and strange rock formations—none of which Jerry wanted to encounter. His destination, Apache Lake, lay west of Theodore Roosevelt Lake, a manmade body of water made possible by the Roosevelt Dam capturing the Salt River's waters. Jerry caught a glimpse of the impressive dam from a distance and then, thankfully, was able to get himself and Fan onto a ferry that delivered them to the southwestern shore of Roosevelt Lake; the ferry saved them a full day's ride.

The sun had just begun its final descent when Jerry made camp near Apache Lake. Not as mammoth as Roosevelt Lake, but the mountain terrain not far in back of them looked equally formidable. Hot, weary to the bone, and crusted with sweat, dirt, and blood, Jerry dismounted, his eyes drawn to the water. As soon as he removed Fan's saddle, he dumped his holster, gun, clothes, and boots in a pile, and headed straight into the lake, Fan leading the way.

The soothing cool waters of Apache Lake washed away dirt and pain, and it eased the fatigue of a thousand road-weary miles. Several times, Fan submerged herself like a giant sea monster, her head barely above the water, then walked up on the shore and shook. A minute later she walked back into the water and submerged again. It made Jerry laugh. "Feels good, girl?"

Floating on his back, he squinted at the deepening colors of the sky and sunset-tinted clouds. The following day would prove crucial; they had to reach Phoenix—which Jerry hoped was no more than forty miles to the west. Fan's shoes had to be replaced, and she needed a full day's rest. She needed a lot more than a day, but that was all they could spare. They had come a thousand miles in thirty-three days. Tired and sore, tougher and wiser, Jerry realized the most dangerous obstacle they would face still lay ahead—the Mojave Desert.

They played in the water until hunger drove Jerry out. He dried Fan down and fed her. Exhausted, she ate her grain and then went to sleep. He was equally worn out; too tired to hunt even though he could have had his pick of small game. Jerry ate beans and left-over biscuits, and a can of peaches for dessert—sustenance, not pleasure. A canyon wren in a nearby paloverde tree sang him a sweet song while he ate. Jerry applied Bag Balm on his leg and other scratches, and then hoping it would relieve his fatigue, made a pot of coffee and drank two cups. The end of another day, Jerry stretched out on his bedroll, his mind skitting over a myriad of images.

Like the skies of New Mexico, the Arizona night sky sparkled with millions of stars and a golden moon. Jerry glanced in Fan's direction, just out of the fire's light. *What a champ she is, such a big heart.* He thought of the barber's question. "Why are you risking your neck?" He wasn't only risking his neck; he was risking Fan's as well. One factor loomed larger each day and now was his overriding concern. Jerry hadn't acknowledged it until the Salt River incident.

The bet and his original plan, to travel light in a race against time, was based on a ride the length of a trail drive—fifteen hundred miles. Distance-wise their ride would be about the same but there was a crucial difference; on Rolla and Frank's drives they'd had a remuda of ten to twenty horses, depending on how many cowboys. Wranglers switched mounts everyday and rarely, if ever, did a horse put in the kind of duty Fan was enduring. Also, their drives were much slower-paced because speed was dictated by the herd, so they covered fewer miles in a day.

Jerry admonished himself for not realizing he should have brought another horse, or even two, so Fan would not have to carry his weight day in and day out. She had shown the strength and stamina of five horses but it wasn't fair to her; Fan could very well end up lame because of a bet. She needed to regain her strength and recover from muscle fatigue, the signs of which had become too obvious to ignore. He noted that she didn't roll in the dirt after he dried her off, but even worse, when she had the chance tonight, the horse that loved to eat was too tired to graze.

Jerry felt exhaustion, too. His entire body ached, pushed to its limit with no opportunity to recover. Fatigue aside, Jerry could not fall asleep; he felt restless and in need to feel close to his family. Away from civilization with only the moon, the stars, and a sleeping horse for company, writing to them was the only way he knew. Jerry retrieved his pencil and writing pad and addressed a letter to his mother, father, and brothers. He wrote about the beautiful country he had seen; he told them that the Rocky Mountains were majestic enough to be the throne of God. He didn't mention desperados or stampeding mustangs, or nearly drowning in the Salt River; nor did he write how grateful he felt to be alive and in one piece.

He described how he felt about their journey. *"I feel like this trip has changed me, made me look at everything differently. One thing for sure, I won't take simple things for granted any more—good food, neat smells, being clean, a soft bed, and having people around who love me. Every day brings a challenge, something that I've never faced. There's no one to rely on but me, so I have to find a way to meet it. I understand now, Dad, why you have always stressed being strong and responsible. This is not a journey for quitters."*

Jerry wrote a sentence or two to each brother; the last part of the letter he addressed to his mother. He wrote "I love you, Mom" and then paused, realizing that at twenty years of age, except for a "Love, Jerry" on a Valentine or Mother's Day card, he had never before written those words to her. *"I want to thank you, Mom, for urging me to take this ride, for teaching me the importance of being honest and standing for something. I've seen the results of that first-hand on this trip."* Jerry underlined that, thinking about how honest William and Elias had been to return Fan, his Winchester, and all his belongings. *"I can picture you in the kitchen cooking dinner and lining the boys up to turn their hands over to prove that they had washed good. I hope the Alberta peaches on my favorite tree will still be ripe when I get back and that you'll make me a peach cobbler—I think I could eat the whole thing. Tell Dad I'll want some of his ice cream on top. I love you all."*

Just as Jerry started to sign the letter, he heard a horrendous scream and then Fan's terrified whinny. The sound resonated off the rocks and echoed out over the water, instantly changing his fatigue to fight readiness. Heart pounding, he grabbed the Winchester, leapt to his feet and took off in Fan's direction, the pages of his letter falling forgotten on the sand.

Out away from the firelight, Jerry saw the mountain lion, thirty feet away on a flat rock above Fan. Silhouetted against the moon was a male lion, six feet long, a hundred-fifty pounds of lithe power crouched and ready to spring. Fan was rearing and kicking wildly. The cat flattened his ears and growled, mouth open wide, flashing powerful teeth. In that blink of an eye, Jerry's world went into slow motion. He barely heard the low ominous snarl rattling in the back of the cat's throat—or Fan's terrified whinnies. He stood mesmerized by the cat's beauty and power—until it growled again. The guttural sound jolted him to action; he fired two shots in the air. The cat leaped off the rock and disappeared into the night, leaving Jerry to stare after him. Legs trembling, he fired another shot in the air for good measure. Still fighting her tether, Fan was desperate to escape from the enemy. Jerry dropped the rifle, holstered his Colt, and grabbed her rope with both hands. She was all right, terrified but not harmed. "Easy, girl, easy," he said. It took a full five minutes of soothing and Jerry's steady hand to calm her. Fan blew and snorted and stiffened her front legs, alert and ready to bolt. When she finally quieted, Jerry coiled up the picket rope and brought her closer to the campfire on the other side of his bedroll.

"It's okay now, Fan. Tell you what, I'll read you my letter." He spoke to her in a quiet, calm voice and then looked around for the pages. They were nowhere to be found. "I thought I wrote a letter." Fan nickered and Jerry stroked her muzzle, for a moment wondering if he actually did write a letter or just dreamed he had. His boot found the broken pencil sticking out of the sand. "I did write a long letter! The breeze must have blown it in the fire."

Jerry reloaded the Colt, put more wood on the fire, and then stretched out on his bedroll. The second he closed his eyes, he visualized the cat's golden eyes staring straight at him. "If I live to be a hundred, I'll never forget those eyes," he said to the stars. The Winchester lay across him, ready. Jerry swore not to sleep, knowing sadly that if the cat came back, he would have no choice but to kill it.

– 22 –

Horse Sense

The Arizona Republic, June 6, 1946
• *Black Marketing Thrives in Food-Pinched Nation* •
• *Chicago Housewives Chase Bread Trucks Shouting Bids* •
• *U.S. Farm Prices Reach Highest Levels Since 1920* •

Jerry now began the day half expecting a calamity. He figured that way if one didn't happen it was a bonus, and if it did he would be ready. He thought back to the cowboy who posed atop Fan for the *Guthrie Daily Leader* the day before he left. Foreman of the Bar R, rodeo rider, proficient handler of horses, he had considered himself a cowboy. Jerry shook his head and smiled. *What a greenhorn I was.*

After her two dips in Apache Lake, Fan seemed fresh when they left at sun-up the following morning. It soon became obvious, however, that they had a new enemy—the heat. By the time they stopped for lunch, it had to be a hundred degrees, maybe more. When he removed Fan's saddle, her back felt dangerously hot and it was soaked. She rolled in the dirt to soothe her skin.

To the south across the reservoir system of lakes, the Superstition Mountains stood tall against the skyline like ancient fortifications. A land of red-hued monoliths carved into strange shapes by the elements, fragrant desert flora, and giant saguaros—prickly monuments in their own right. It teamed with javelinas, black-tailed jack rabbits, chukars, deer, and puma. To Jerry, the Superstition Mountains meant rugged terrain and daunting temperatures. He used the sun and his compass to navigate through and around sun-baked canyons north of the string of lakes. Picking up a path, a long-ago sheep trail judging by the hoof prints and sparse vegetation, Jerry kept a look-out for rattlers as Fan walked along at a steady pace. He hoped they would soon be out of these hills and onto the flat, open desert where there would be a breeze, albeit a hot one.

Fan slowed and came to a stop. Red lights went off in Jerry's head. What now? He quickly dismounted and checked her. She didn't have any mucus and her breathing sounded fine. Jerry knelt and checked Fan's shoes. Finding nothing wrong, he glanced around for signs of potential trouble. "What's the matter, Fan?"

Up ahead the arroyo narrowed at the entrance but from what Jerry could see, it looked like it flared out again within fifteen or twenty feet. Horses did not have good depth perception; perhaps she felt unsure about the opening. The straight-up walls reminded Jerry of the draw where the stampede happened, except this one was twice as high and much narrower. Could Fan be remembering that? Jerry walked ahead and checked; nothing appeared unusual.

This trail led straight to Phoenix and following it, they had a chance to reach the outskirts of the city by dusk. If they backtracked or significantly altered their route to ride south and follow the highway on the other side of the lakes, they would lose an entire day—maybe more. They were less than a yard from being through the narrow opening. Jerry unrolled Fan's lead rope and walked through it, tugging her rope for her to follow. "What is it, girl? Are you still spooked because of the cat?"

She splayed her front legs and stood stiff and straight, refusing to budge. The blazing sun beat down, radiating off the rocks searing them from all sides, broiling and baking them. He felt like they were in an oven; he was soaked with sweat, and Fan completely lathered. "Come on, don't be mule-headed. We've come through a half-a-dozen canyons like this. Don't do this to me, okay?" No amount of pleading or tugging could get Fan to move, and Jerry began to lose patience. Nothing appeared to be out of the ordinary that he could see. He pulled himself back into the saddle and listened again. Hearing nothing, Jerry spurred Fan with the hand-tooled spurs he wore but had yet to use on this trip. "Giddyup, Fan. Come on. Don't be stubborn." Fan lowered and shook her head; she whinnied and side-stepped, stubbornly refusing to move. Jerry dug the spurs in harder. "Dammitall, Fan, let's go!" His shout slammed back at him off the walls, reverberating through the canyon. Fan whinnied and reared up. Caught by surprise, Jerry gripped her sides and had to hang on to keep from getting dumped out of the saddle.

It started as a low rumble, small rocks raining down and then a second later, a boulder cracked loose from the wall above and crashed onto the trail in front of them. Jerry hung on as Fan jerked back and whirled around and took off in a full run. It took everything he could do to stop her once they reached a wide spot away from the rock slide. "Whoa, girl, come on, whoa!" He reined her in. "Damn, I think you'd run all the way back to Oklahoma if I let you." Jerry brought her to a halt in the shade of a giant saguaro and turned her around.

He held Fan steady and watched as boulders and rocks cascaded down, a thick cloud of red dust billowing up. When it cleared, the canyon entrance had disappeared, replaced by a pile of boulders twice as high as Fan. Jerry sat motionless in the saddle staring at the rubble and listening as small rocks plinked down on the pile. He knew horses had a sixth sense, but this was the first evidence of it he had ever witnessed.

"You just saved our lives." He dismounted and checked Fan's flanks where he had used the spurs. A bloody line showed where his spurs had broken her skin. "You knew something wasn't right and I wouldn't listen." Jerry ran his fingers across the scrape. "I'm sorry, girl. I'll put something on it, don't want you any madder at me than you already are." Jerry fetched the Bag Balm and applied it to the scratches on both flanks. He removed the beautiful hand-tooled spurs and put them in his saddlebag. *Never again.*

They backtracked for a ways and then Jerry dismounted and tied

Fan to a paloverde tree at the base of a low rise. Keeping his eye out for rattlers, he climbed over and around rocks and cacti to the top. From the vantage point, he spotted another arroyo that looked to be parallel to the one now closed off. *It's worth a try.* He climbed back down, untied Fan, and led her for a short distance until she seemed settled down. He walked until he could see an opening back onto the trail, then mounted up and, this time, let Fan determine whether it was safe to walk through. She evidently thought so, for she trotted into the arroyo as though she had forgotten the rock slide altogether. It took another hour to get out of the hills and into the open desert.

Jerry and Fan rode west, chasing the sun, gratefully reaching the outskirts of Phoenix just as the sun disappeared. A huge stockyard on the northern edge of the city loomed right in front of them. He rode between rows of tall pole barns into the cool dimness until he located the office. The stockyard manager had been a cowboy once—a hundred pounds ago. A Texan, he said, out of Dallas. White-haired, with a full beard neatly trimmed, he reminded Jerry of pictures he'd seen of Bill Cody. The manager informed Jerry that the stockyard was part of the Maricopa County rodeo circuit. Its rest rooms and showers were for rodeo participants who did just what Jerry intended to do, stay with his horse. "Y'all are welcome to stay as long as you need. The hay ain't moldy and the water's pure. You just passin' through?"

"You might say that," Jerry said, and gave him a short explanation of his journey and the bet. He desperately wanted a shower, some hot food and a good night's sleep.

"Well, I've heard it all now—ridin' half-way cross the country on a bet." The manager shook his head, his look of disbelief turning to alarm when he spied Fan. "You'd best take care of your mare, cowboy. She looks as worn out as you do. I'll have Tony bring you some hay and grain. Pay when you leave."

"Thank you. By the way, do you know a good place close by to eat?"

Jerry's question brought a belly laugh from the manager, waking

Fan. "You asked the right person." He patted his stomach. "The Stockman, just down the block. They got the biggest and best steak in Phoenix."

Fan got her cool bath first. "You've earned this and a whole lot more." Jerry dried her down. The stableman, like Ernie, the fairgrounds care-taker in Clovis, acted concerned about Fan. He brought her hay and grain and, after she had eaten her fill, he fed her two apples when he learned they were her favorite treat. Jerry showered and put on his clean shirt. He brushed and reshaped his Stetson as best he could, his teeth marks unfortunately forever imprinted in the brim. Jerry gave the stableman a dollar to keep an eye on Fan and his gear.

"*Gracias, mi amigo.* I will take good care of this very tired horse. Would you like me to show you the dormitory? We have bunks you could use."

"No, thanks. After what my horse has been through, I'd rather stay close by. Besides, I forgot what a real bed feels like. I don't want to get spoiled."

Fan had become much more to Jerry than a means to get to California; they were in this together. Earlier today, her horse sense had saved his life, and yesterday he had saved her from the mountain lion. Fan's well-being meant as much to him as his own. As soon as he saw her resting and he felt confident that she was in good hands, Jerry followed the manager's directions to the Stockman's Bar and Restaurant.

– 23 –

The Birthday Party

The Guthrie Daily Leader, June 6, 1946
• *Higher Grain Prices Mean Famine Relief Abroad, Less Meat For U.S.* •
• *Oklahoma Vets Get Trade & Ag Training in New Program* •
• *Alaskans Vote in Favor Of Statehood* •

"Vearl, would you go fetch the boys from the bunkhouse? Dad and Frank are here," Edna Van Meter said to her husband. She glanced out the window at Frank and her father getting out of Rolla's Chevy truck. Both were laughing at something as they headed toward the house; Edna marveled at them. In two days on June 8, Rolla would turn seventy-six; Frank's eighty-sixth birthday was in October yet they still moved like young men. "They are going to ride together in heaven, those two," she said to Vearl as he went to get the boys.

"I smell some good fried chicken," Frank said when he came through the door.

"If you want some, cowboy, you'll have to check your hat and guns at the door." Edna gave each of them a kiss on the cheek. She noted Frank had spiffed up, as Rolla called it, and she smiled an acknowledgment to her father. "Happy birthday, Dad."

"Thanks, Edna. Since it's my birthday, it'd be fine with me if you hold off feedin' this varmint. He's been givin' me grief, all day."

Frank took off his holster. "I'll put my guns in the car, Edna, but pay Rolla here no mind. He thinks he's smarter only because he's havin' a birthday. I told him I'm always gonna be older and smarter 'n him. You back me up on this."

Edna laughed. "I am not going to get in the line of fire between Rolla Goodnight and Pistol Pete. I'd be the one to end up full of holes."

"Me against Slow-draw Goodnight?" Frank grinned in Rolla's direction. "Be right back." He closed the door on Rolla's indignant glance.

All the food on the table had either come from the Van Meter victory garden or from their flock of chickens: four fryers, twenty potatoes served mashed with homemade butter and cream, and four quarts of canned green beans. The entire family took part in raising the chickens which they sold along with fresh eggs to the stores in Guthrie. Their large garden and five-acre orchard produced enough vegetables and fruits to feed their five boys and fill the cellar for winter. They shared their bounty with neighbors and, during the summer, made extra money from a roadside stand. During the Depression, Edna gave away more food than she sold.

After their meal, Vearl helped Edna serve the birthday cake.

"Tell us the tarantula story, Grandpa," Billy said. Conversation stopped and Billy, David, and Byron leaned forward in anticipation.

Rolla and Frank nodded at each other, about to tell one of their favorite trail stories. Rolla started. "Well, Frank 'n me had our hands full. We was drivin' this herd of longhorns along a dry riverbed. Everything seemed to be going fine when all of a sudden the poundin' of the cattle's hooves made all these tarantulas come up outta the sand and start crawlin' up the longhorns' legs."

"Whooee!" Frank chimed in. "Them cows went crazy, snortin' and jumpin' and kickin'. Next thing we knew they started stampedin' and for a while, we thought they was going to end up in Mexico before we could bring 'em to a stop."

"How did you stop them?" David said.

Rolla laughed. "Why, expert-like, of course. We—"

The telephone rang in the middle of the rescue. Edna rose and answered it. "Yes, I'll accept the charges." The excitement in her voice quieted the others. "It's Jerry. He's calling collect from Arizona!"

* * *

Jerry watched patrons file in and out of the Stockman's Bar and Restaurant as the operator put through his call and asked if his mother would accept the charges. "Jerry, it's wonderful to hear your voice. Where in Arizona are you?"

"I'm in Phoenix, Mom. It's wonderful to hear you, too. Sounds like you have a house full. Who's there?"

"Everybody but you and your brother Jimmy. We're celebrating Dad's birthday. It's on Saturday, but we are celebrating early and he and Frank are here for dinner. We were just having birthday cake. You couldn't have called at a better time."

Jerry closed his eyes. "What kind of cake?" His mother chuckled.

"Chocolate, the moist one I make with mayonnaise. It's so good to talk to you, son. I wish you were here."

"So do I." Jerry could almost taste the cake. "I feel terrible, Mom. I forgot about Grandpa's birthday."

"Don't worry. Hearing from you is the perfect gift."

Jerry talked to every member of his family, the longest long distance call he'd ever made. Rolla got on the line and asked if the wild china trees had leafed out yet in the Palo Duro when Jerry was there. Jerry heard his grandfather sigh when he told him they had. "Happy birthday, Grandpa. Wish I could be there to celebrate with you."

"I appreciate that, son. You havin' a good time on your adventure?" Rolla didn't talk on a telephone very often, so when he did he felt it necessary to shout. Jerry held the phone away from his ear.

"I am, Grandpa, certain times more than others. I made it into

Phoenix this evening. We're going to rest up all day tomorrow then head out over the desert early Saturday."

"Fancy's okay now? You need money? If you do, just say so 'cause I know how to wire you some through Western Union."

"No, I'm doing okay on money. I'm fine and Fan is okay, just tired. Those silver dollars you had me bring along did come in handy. Glad you told me to do that."

"We sure enjoyed your letter. Write us another one if you can. Before I forget, I ran into your friend, Carlton Schier in Marshall the other day. He said to tell you he and everybody in town is rootin' for you. Wait a minute, Frank is grabbin' at the telephone, the old fart. I either have to let him talk to you or shoot him."

Jerry pushed his hat back, shaking with silent laughter at the two of them. Noise followed in the background then Frank's voice came on the line. "Thanks for the book, Jerry. I started readin' it the next day. Tell me, did you really say fill your hand, you son of a…?"

"I did. It came out natural as can be. How you doing, Frank?"

"Well, I'll be dawg. I'm spit-fire fine, Jerry, and plenty proud of you."

Frank wanted to hear all about Fan. Jerry told him about the rockslide and how she had sensed it. "I knew she'd do right by you. I'm glad you're makin' the trip on her. Smart mare, she's got horse sense."

"Right this minute I'm thinking she's got more sense than me. You and Grandpa gonna stay in Guthrie tonight?"

"Yeah, your Mama talked us into to it. The boys want me to listen to The Cisco Kid with 'em on the radio. After that, Roy Rogers and Dale Evans is on with that Gabby Hayes fella. The boys say he's tryin' to imitate me. I told 'em, slim chance."

Jerry asked to speak to his mother again before he hung up. "I wrote you a long letter, but…got side-tracked by something and it blew into the fire."

"What a shame. I would have liked that. Are you all right, Jerry? You sound tired."

"I am tired but we're going to rest up tomorrow. This country is really something, Mom. I'll try to write while I'm here so you'll get it next week."

Jerry could not bring himself to say aloud the things he had put in the letter. After he reluctantly hung up, he stood staring at the telephone, hating to sever the connection to the people he loved most. The call buoyed his spirits but at the same time brought an acute attack of loneliness. Jerry could close his eyes and picture everyone sitting around the big table in the Guthrie kitchen. He could smell the fried chicken and chocolate cake and hear the laughter.

His remedy for loneliness: he ordered the biggest steak on the menu from a pretty waitress who called him "cowboy" when she told him to sit anywhere he liked. "Want anything to drink with that steak?" she asked.

"I sure do, the tallest, coldest beer you've got."

Every time she went by Jerry's table, the waitress stopped and visited, asking where he was from, finding out a little more about him with each stop. When Jerry mentioned a few of his adventures, she made him promise to tell her his story from the beginning. On her next stop she delivered a huge green salad smothered in buttermilk dressing. "My name is Sheila and, from the sounds of it, you haven't had one of these in a while. It's on the house, except you have to tell me your name and why you're making this ride. I have a few minutes."

"Jerry Van Meter, from Guthrie, Oklahoma." He tore through the salad; it tasted as good as the steak. Talking between bites, he told her about the bet and the journey. Sheila listened attentively and stayed until he finished his dinner. "Thanks for the salad and the company," Jerry said as he got up to leave. He left a big tip on the table.

"Anytime," she said and followed him to the door. "I hope you'll come back."

Buoyed by the good dinner and Sheila's attention, Jerry left with a spring in his step. He bought four shoes for Fan on his way back to the stockyards. The following morning, with the stableman's help, he trimmed and cleaned Fan's hooves and replaced her worn shoes. Jerry watered and fed her and she fell asleep again within a few minutes.

The stableman shook his head. "She *es muy consado, señor,* very tired indeed."

"So am I, but I've got some shopping to do before I rest. And I'd like to see a little of this city." Jerry took a bus into downtown Phoenix. Because the stockyards were on the eastern edge of the city, the ride offered Jerry the opportunity to see the contrast in landscapes. He passed acres of tiny box-like houses, then businesses fronting on traffic-filled streets followed by more homes and more businesses. Phoenix looked to be a sprawling collection of districts and neighborhoods strung together by lanes of asphalt over what not long ago had been desert.

The city stretched outward gobbling up landscape from a busy nucleus that, itself, was very old. Bustling even in the mid-day heat, it seemed to radiate energy; cars and people in motion, busy stores, shoppers with their arms laden with packages, and businessmen with briefcases. Phoenix seemed to represent what Jimmy Wakely told his grandfather and Frank; Jerry couldn't help but wonder if Wakely was also right about family farms and ranches dying.

Guess I'll find out. Signs of the war were still evident; men and women in uniform, and war posters advertising movies at the theaters. Jerry had to stare at how civilian women were dressed—not in dresses but in long pants with military-looking tops. He strolled along glancing in department store windows. Female mannequins dressed the same way, sloppy joe sweaters or military-type jackets with epaulets. He had to smile; his mother would never wear long pants. Trim, always "properly dressed" as she called it, Edna considered a hat and gloves necessary attire when going out. The thought of her dressed in the clothes on the mannequins made Jerry smile. Men's suits looked like a civilian version of their military counterpart: double-breasted jacket, full pants with cuffs and, at thirty dollars, almost a week's wages. Money aside, Jerry could not fathom when anyone in Phoenix would need a jacket.

He bought a new pair of Denim Riders and then stopped for an uptown lunch. He took a seat at the counter and ordered a hamburger and a salad with buttermilk dressing, hoping it would be as good as the one at the Stockman's Bar. On the radio behind the bar, Bill Stern was interviewing Cleveland's star pitcher, Bob Feller. The bartender turned the volume up so Jerry could listen. By the time he finished his lunch, Stern had ended the interview. "What a guy," the bartender said. "Enlisted in the navy at the height of his career. Highly decorated, you know."

"I know." Jerry did know all about Bob Feller, who was his brother Billy's hero. Billy collected pictures and newspaper clippings of Feller in his navy uniform as an antiaircraft gunner on the *U.S.S. Alabama*. His favorite picture was of Feller in his Cleveland uniform when he joined the team as the youngest player in Cleveland's history. Billy wanted to be a major league pitcher; at the very least he wanted to see Feller pitch now that he had returned to Cleveland.

"Yeah, quite a guy," Jerry said and paid his bill. Bob Feller made him think of the navy. Riding the bus back, Jerry wondered about his squadron. Where were his buddies now? What were they flying? It had been a long time since he'd thought about them or the navy. When Jerry reached the stockyard and walked up to Fan's stall, he found her asleep. He could hardly keep his own eyes open, but he kept his promise to write to his family. Frank and Rolla must have shared their letter with his mother because she scolded him for not telling her everything. This time he wrote about the bad parts as well as the good; the rockslide and how scared he'd been in the Salt River when he became separated from Fan. He described meeting William and Elias and told his mother how they helped him.

After finishing his letters, Jerry slept until hunger awakened him. He gravitated back to the Stockman's Bar and Restaurant—whether for the excellent food or the pretty waitress, he wasn't sure. Sheila greeted him with a dazzling smile. She wore her dark hair very short and curly—different from the women in Oklahoma, a big city look, he decided. It seemed every woman in downtown Phoenix had a similar hairdo, and on Sheila it looked good. Friday night turned out to be *twenty-five-cents-a-drink night* for anyone in the military or recently out of the service, which pretty much took in all the men and women in the place.

The jukebox blared out one hit after another and, after a month of silence, the music and laughter sounded good. Somebody must have really liked the Andrews Sisters' *Don't Sit Under the Apple Tree* because it played three times in a row. The only bad part with the place being so crowded, Sheila didn't have any time to visit. She did remember the salad though. By ten o'clock every barstool was occupied, and a dozen couples were dancing, jitterbugging one minute then dancing to a slow song the next. Jerry stayed around until the crowd thinned.

Sheila approached his table. "I'm glad you stuck around. I hate that I've been so busy we haven't had a chance to talk. Didn't you tell me you were leaving tomorrow?"

"Before daylight in the morning. I'm kind of worried about the heat."

"I wish you didn't have to go so soon. I work the late-shift tomorrow. So I don't have to come in until five o'clock." She looked at him invitingly. Jerry's heart sank. He knew without giving it a second thought that he couldn't stay. If he tried his hardest and didn't make it, at least he'd given it his all. If he stayed to spend the day with a pretty girl and didn't make it, he would never forgive himself.

"I'd like nothing better, but I can't," Jerry said, unable to mask his regret.

"I understand, but you can do one thing for me before you go. You can dance with me."

"It's been a long time since I danced—" Jerry started to make excuses and then realized what he'd be turning down. "Yes, ma'am," he said. She led him onto the empty dance floor. Jerry put a nickel in the jukebox. "Pick whatever song you want."

She chose *Somebody Else is Taking My Place*. They danced, oblivious of the small crowd watching them. Sheila put both arms around Jerry's neck and sighed contentedly with her cheek against his. When the song finished, Sheila kissed Jerry goodbye. It made leaving all that much harder.

– 24 –

Mother Nature's Frying Pan

The Wickenburg Sun, June 9, 1946
• *Boy Scouts Collect Canned Goods for Starving Europeans* •
• *Strict Measures Result from Arizona's Worst Drought Since 1921* •
• *May and June Precipitation Zero, Temperatures Reach 106* •

Jerry and Fan rode out of Phoenix before dawn on June 9, headed for the Colorado River and California. The stableman, when he'd said goodbye the previous evening, suggested they find shade in the hottest part of the day and travel as much as they could before daylight and after sunset. Common sense told Jerry to follow that advice.

The homes on the northern fringe of the sprawling city looked like small, rectangular brick boxes with low roofs and shallow yards. *Hot,* Jerry thought as he rode by. Moonlight glinted off their silent dark windows, opened to catch the desert breeze. A few vigilant dogs barked at the shadowy passersby. A lone porch light went on, then off, and the neighborhood became quiet and dark again. Jerry and Fan reached the open desert hours before the sun came up. Not long after it rose, he realized the stableman's suggestion would be difficult to follow.

Shade, in the form of mesquite trees and bushes, could hardly be found. And shade or no shade, the unrelenting heat enveloped them like a blanket, rising off the sand in shimmering waves, baking from beneath and searing from above. The air was so hot it seemed to cook from within. By the time they stopped for their first rest at eight o'clock, Fan was completely lathered and Jerry was soaking wet. The early sun's rays came from behind him, but its glare bounced off the sand, blinding like sun on snow. He thought about his trampled, discarded Stetson; Fan would look ridiculous with it on her head, but he wished he had saved it for her anyway.

Their first evening brought a gift, cloud cover that blocked the sun and created huge patches of shade on the parched earth. Thunderheads began to form as Jerry and Fan approached the Hassayampa River south of Wickenburg. The riverbed's gouged-out banks spoke of past storms and raging torrents, but now it had barely enough water for desert creatures to survive. After thirty miles in suffocating heat, Jerry decided to make camp. The storm held the promise of rain, and the stableman had warned him that Arizona rainstorms created instant torrents in washes and riverbeds.

Dismounting near a group of mesquite trees close to the river, Jerry unpacked, keeping his eye on the intensifying storm. The wind picked up as the sky darkened. Thunder rumbled, and flashes of lightning streaked through the black clouds. With the blinding sun covered, the desert's colors brightened and its fragrance came to life. A trio of prairie dogs near the river's bank stood at attention, waiting expectantly.

Jerry felt his skin cool and his lungs expand with the promise of moisture-laden air. Lightning flashed, and Jerry, Fan, and their prairie dog neighbors were treated to an all-encompassing cloudburst. A lengthy deluge, the downpour swelled the water level in the river and Jerry had to scramble to replace Fan's bridle with a halter as she determinedly headed into the stream.

There were at least two givens about Fan: her endless appetite and her love of water. Many times in Oklahoma when she spied a body of water, Fan headed into it undeterred despite Jerry's efforts to stop her. This river proved to be no exception: she waded right in and began to drink. If she drank slowly, Fan could take in five gallons at one time without foundering. She thankfully did exactly that—drank slowly—even though their ride had been long and hot.

Her crisp brown and white colors brightened after Jerry waded in and washed the crusted sweat from her coat. She stretched her neck and shook as he scooped the cool water over her—a sign she liked it. Fan stayed in the river a long time but when she came out, she rolled in the dirt, first on one side and then the other. Afterward, she looked as dirty as she had before the storm.

"You look terrible." Fan stared back at him, chomping contentedly on the rolled oats he put in front of her. Jerry chuckled at her happy face: thirst-quenched, cool, dirt-covered, and eating. "Frank was right, you are one great horse."

By the time Jerry cleaned himself up in the river, the storm had rumbled past and Fan was asleep. She had become a savvy traveler, eating and drinking when offered, seeking out what little shade could be found, and sleeping at the first opportunity. The storm provided plentiful water for Jerry to refill his containers and, afterward, to wash his sweat-soaked clothes and Fan's blanket. Everything had faded from being washed often and dried in the bright sun.

The next morning the heat returned, but for a short while the desert and everything in it felt and looked refreshed. The moist sand lent an earthy fragrance to the morning; the air crackled with freshness. Jerry breathed deep with enjoyment, but both pleasures were short-lived, lasting only until the sun came up.

Jerry and Fan skirted the base of the Big Horn Mountains, mesquite-covered hills that rose abruptly from the flat desert expanse. At the end of their second day, ten miles east of Quartzsite, they intersected Highway 10. Jerry couldn't resist looking back at the two lanes of asphalt. It narrowed with the distance into a shimmering thread, finally becoming no more than a speck on the horizon. Jerry patted Fan's wet neck. "Look how far we've come." Cars with canvas water bags hanging by a thick rope from their door handle or hood ornament rumbled by on the highway, Most of the drivers honked a greeting and Jerry would then see hands appear through open windows, waving at them. Without fail, every head in every car turned to stare, curious at what a horse and rider would be doing in the middle of this God-forsaken landscape. Several cars stopped, the people offering water and asking if they could help. Jerry accepted the water, not bothering to explain their presence. If he had told them, they would have thought he was crazy. *Maybe I am.*

The town of Quartzsite consisted of an intersection of two ribbons of asphalt that came out of nowhere, met in the middle of nowhere, and then stretched into nowhere in all four directions. Businesses on two of the corners and a few attendant shacks provided the only sign that life existed at this crossroads. Quartzsite and its surroundings, Jerry thought, made the Texas Panhandle look like a park.

The farther west they rode, the more desert-like and sparse the vegetation became. Ocotillo, creosote bushes, mesquite, chaparral, and prickly cacti stood as proud survivors of the heat and meager rainfall. Jerry thought back to the beginning of the desert below the Mogollon Rim with its mild temperatures and plenty of water and shade. Those were aberrations for any geography labeled *desert. This* was the desert he so dreaded when he had planned this trip, landscape that threatened to bake the life out of anyone or anything with the audacity to try and cross it.

The body reacted to extreme heat by sweating profusely to cool it. It meant that Fan stayed soaking wet all the time and Jerry did too. He recognized the symptoms: cramping muscles, fatigue, and limbs that felt like lead. Jerry made a point to eat salt every morning and he began adding it to Fan's food every other day. Instead of three rests per day, he upped it to four. He realized that the constant sweat-soaked saddle blanket against her back, when combined with the tremendous heat, invited trouble. Each time they stopped he took her saddle off and dried her back with a towel. He fed Fan sparingly but often, the same with water. It was important to keep the tissues of her mouth moist. As miserable as conditions were, when they camped after the sun went down, she rolled like a puppy in the dirt—a good sign.

They started each morning well before dawn and traveled long after the sun went down. If Jerry could find shade in the hottest part of the day, they stopped and slept, then rode again until they were too tired to ride any farther. The nights cooled off only slightly, ten to twelve degrees less than the one-hundred-degree-plus days, but the absence of the blinding sun made it seem cooler.

Late in the afternoon their fourth day out of Phoenix, Jerry and Fan reached the Colorado River. Ehrenberg, Arizona, occupied the east side of the state line, Blythe, California, the west. Jerry rode toward the *Agricultural Inspection Station* sign with an overwhelming sense of accomplishment; day forty and they were 1,245-five miles from Guthrie. They had ten days to cover the 255 five miles to Hollywood. Heat, fatigue, sweat, hunger, his constant companions for the last few weeks, momentarily disappeared, swept away by a rush of pride. They had crossed two states and part of two others. They were at California's doorstep.

"Look at that, Fan. Hollywood, here we come. We'll follow the highway from here on in and be there in plenty of time." Fan's ears didn't twitch or move. Jerry squeezed her with his knees. "Hey, you awake?" She flicked her ears a couple of times. "That's more like it."

Up ahead a sign, *Welcome to California,* hung from the side of the closest building. In the adjacent parking lot, a half dozen 1941 Packards were lined up diagonally side-by-side in a black and white display of authority. Black front and rear, white roof and mid-section, each car had a California Highway Patrol seal painted in the middle of the doors and a spotlight adjacent to the driver's window. Huge diesel rigs were also parked in the lot and Jerry could see uniformed CHP officers moving silently around them checking tires and brakes. When he saw the officers' pistols and wide belts lined with bullets, his smile vanished.

Jerry stopped in front of a uniformed guard, as wide as he was no-doubt tall, sitting in the shade of the building underneath the welcome sign. The expression on his face looked anything but welcoming as he stood up and signaled for Jerry to dismount. The guard spoke in an officious tone, his words matching his demeanor. "Just where do you think you're going on that horse, mister?"

Jerry led Fan into the shade of the building. "We're on our way to Hollywood…sir."

"Not on a horse, you're not."

Jerry's heart sank. "What do you mean? I don't understand."

"If you'd paid attention to the signs along the highway, you wouldn't have to ask."

"We came across the desert, didn't reach the highway until Quar—"

"At the present time," he interrupted, "there is an interdiction in affect that bans bringing horses into the state of California." He spoke in an exasperated sing-song voice.

Jerry wondered what kind of problem it could be, and how widespread to prompt such a ban. The guard rattled off the name of a disease and, deep in thought, Jerry didn't catch it. It didn't sound like anything he had ever heard of, but he wasn't about to ask the guard to repeat it. He needed to know how long this interdiction would last. "Exactly what does that mean? Is it just today or this week?"

The guard smirked. "It means there's no way you're going to cross *this* border on *that* horse. And it's not going to be over in the next few days or weeks." He took a long look at Fan, Jerry's eyes following his gaze. Her head hung low and her eyes were half-closed; the exhausted mare had fallen asleep. *He thinks she's sick.*

"You'd better go back where you came from, mister. And don't even *think* of sneaking across. If they catch you," he motioned at the CHP officers, "they'll impound your horse and quarantine it. Who knows when, or *if*, you'd ever get it back." The guard stared at them, his arms folded over his protruding stomach. "Well?"

"Thanks for letting me know," he said, trying not to let his anger show. Jaw clenched tight, Jerry pulled himself back up in the saddle and turned Fan around. "What a grump. Sure as hell the wrong guy to put under a welcome sign, unless they put him in Quartzsite." That thought made Jerry smile.

When they came to Main Street, Jerry spied a little grocery store, its windows glazed with a fine layer of dust. A huge sycamore tree stood beside the building and cast inviting shade over the sidewalk and weed-covered lot next door. Fan automatically headed for the shade. Jerry wrapped her lead rope around the tree trunk and removed her saddle. "*Now* what do I do?" He leaned against the tree, the guard's voice echoing in his ears... "You're not crossing this border on that horse, mister." But parading through Jerry's mind were images of Rolla and Jimmy shaking hands, Frank handing him his Colt, and the image of Highway 10 out of Quartzsite stretching all the way back to Oklahoma.

Fan had begun eating dry grass. "If I cross the border, I'm breaking the law. If we get caught, I'll lose you, girl. I can't lose you, no matter what." Dispirited, Jerry left Fan and went into the store to buy supplies.

– 25 –

Last Rest Stop for a Hundred Miles

California Highway Patrolman Magazine, June, 1946
• *War Cost Equates to Building $8,000 House For Every US Family* •
• *CHP Patrolmen Take Part in Police Traffic Safety Check* •
• *War Ends CHP's Responsibility for Japanese Relocation Camp Security* •

Jerry came out of the store twenty minutes later to find three boys, between six and ten years old, standing near Fan and whispering to each other. When he walked up, the oldest boy spoke up. "Is this your horse, mister?"

"Sure is," Jerry said. He put Fan's saddle back on and began putting his groceries in the saddle bags.

"It's a real pretty horse, what's its name?"

"The horse is a she and her name is Fan. Do you boys have a horse?"

The youngest boy spoke up, displaying a missing front tooth. "I gotta schtick horse," he said, whistling through the space.

Jerry laughed. "I had a stick horse when I was your age." Retrieving a knife from his jeans pocket, he cut up an apple into wedges. "Would you like to help give Fan something she really likes?"

"Yeah." they said in unison and stepped forward.

"Can I pet her?" the little one asked.

"Hang on a minute. Let's give her the treat first." Jerry placed an apple wedge on each outstretched palm and showed them how to stiffen their fingers downward and together to keep them out of the way. The ten-year-old went first, giggling when Fan removed the apple from his hand. Fan ate the other two slices from upheld palms then all three youngsters wiped their hands down the side of their pants. Each boy tentatively patted Fan's flank. Other than twitching her ears and tail, Fan paid no attention to the youngsters as she ate the rest of the apple.

"I'm gonna have me a horse like that when I grow up," the ten-year-old boasted. "Just like Fan."

Jerry finished his packing as the boys' mother came from across the street to retrieve them. She smiled at Jerry. "I hope they didn't bother you. They're crazy about horses. All they talk about is being cowboys. I'm sure they didn't expect to meet a *real* cowboy today."

Something in the way she said "real cowboy," with a touch of admiration in her tone, made Jerry straighten up and stand taller. "No bother, my pleasure, ma'am." Jerry touched the brim of his Stetson and winked at the boys. "Bye, cowboys. Thanks for helping with Fan." Something about the boys reminded him of his brothers. They walked away with their mother, all three talking at once. Jerry heard the ten-year-old say "real cowboy' as he turned and waved.

"Shoot, Fan, I don't want to quit now. We've come too far to not at least put our feet in California. How about it? What do you want?" Fan nudged his hand. "That's easy, you want more apple."

Jerry and Fan circled back through town and then headed north, away from the border crossing. At the northern edge of Ehrenberg, Jerry turned back toward the river. Tents and campers lined the banks of the Colorado. On the river's side in front of each tent, most campers had rigged some type of make-shift shade, varying sizes of canvas stretched and tied to bushes and trees. And under each patch of shade were tables and chairs. In back of the tents Jerry spotted cars with license plates from Minnesota, Iowa, and Wisconsin, each vehicle covered in a thick layer of dust. Noisy children chased each other around and between the tents and cars while their parents fished, or sat in the shade visiting with neighbors. Jerry kept riding for another hour until there were no more campers and the river looked safe to cross. He guessed they were about fifteen miles north of Ehrenberg.

The Colorado wasn't nearly as wide as the Salt River and it looked a great deal less formidable. Flowing by at a more leisurely pace, the water didn't appear to be all that deep. For a second time, Jerry tied everything on top of Fan's saddle and grabbed onto her tail. She waded in. As the cold water started filling his boots, Jerry's heartbeat speeded up. "Here we go again, Fan. How 'bout we stay together this time!" Jerry was prepared for trouble, but no trouble came. He hung onto Fan's tail with his left hand and paddled with his right, this time crossing without incident. The harrowing experience of the Salt River seemed a long time ago.

Jerry looked back across the river. "Well, we made it into California, girl. Not exactly like I planned, but here we are." Jerry spoke almost whispering then looked around. "Why am I being quiet? There isn't another person in sight." He knew why: the mental image of black and white patrol cars and armed patrolmen...*if you're caught, your horse will be impounded.* The thought sent a shiver down his spine.

After he set up camp, Jerry led Fan back into the river. He cleaned her off and took a proper bath himself, then washed his clothes and draped them over a thick bush. With one-hundred-degree air, they would easily dry by bedtime. In Phoenix Jerry had seen men wearing short plaid pants that reached just above the knee. He had snickered at how they looked, and asked the bartender what the world was coming to—grown men wearing little-boy pants.

"They're the latest thing," the bartender told him. "Called Bermuda shorts, and in this heat they aren't such a bad idea."

"I'm gonna make me a pair of Bermuda shorts, Fan." Jerry cut the remaining leg off of his ruined jeans. She observed him putting them on while she grazed near the water's edge. "Hey, I don't want any snickering on your part, lady. These jeans and my leg are what kept you from getting barely a scratch sliding down that mountain. Besides, now I'm right up to snuff."

He gave Fan her rolled oats and then walked along the shore, chuckling at how silly he must look in his cut-off jeans and cowboy boots. His leg had healed with only a few scabs left to remind him of his quick trip down the Salt River Canyon trail. A few yards up from camp Jerry found what he was looking for—a boulder protruding into the river. Climbing out on the rock, he held his make-shift fishing pole with one hand and slapped at mosquitoes with the other. Two twelve-inch trout hung from Jerry's line in no time; he could have had a dozen more. The fish were in a feeding frenzy, biting at the pesky insects landing on the water.

Though the sun had set, the air felt stifling; it had to be at least ninety degrees. Fan did not roll in the dirt. She simply drank, ate, and went to sleep. "You look exhausted, Fan. Could you even make it across the desert?"

After his supper, Jerry cleaned his Colt and Winchester and organized his supplies, glancing at Fan as he worked. Disparate feelings, fear of the desert, compassion for Fan, desire to keep his word, all fought for recognition in his mind. At odds with those feelings were his core beliefs, keeping one's word, not giving up when things got tough, everything Jerry had been taught and what he stood for. Emotional dilemma aside, he knew he had to make a decision.

He had planned to cross the desert following alongside Highway 10 into Palm Springs. Doing so would have provided a safety factor: access to water at gas stations, and food at grocery stores along the highway. And help if they did run into trouble. The interdiction made it a far greater challenge. If he decided to forge on, he chanced losing Fan to armed highway patrolmen with bullets on their belts. The truth, if they were to still have a chance at winning, it would come only if they faced the Mojave alone. They would have to head straight across the desert.

Jerry didn't want to make a reckless decision, one based on pride because three little boys that reminded him of his brothers called him a real cowboy. He stared into the darkness toward the desert. He knew well the country behind them; he could only guess what lay ahead. Jerry looked back across the river, hoping he would get a gut feeling of what to do. It looked the same. "Okay, Fan," he spoke quietly to his sleeping horse. "Suppose I say the risk isn't worth it, then what? How's it gonna be to actually turn around and ride back to Oklahoma? A hundred miles of desert ahead, or twelve hundred miles behind us. How much worse could it be?"

The process of mentally following through on both alternatives gave Jerry his answer. A major factor he could not discount, turning around meant giving up. It meant all the hardships they had overcome would count for nothing. Breaking the law or not, Jerry admitted he could not go back. *This is not a journey for quitters.* He had written that in a letter to his family and, within those seven words, lay a fundamental truth Jerry Van Meter meant to honor.

Once he made the decision, he decided something else. Weight and strength-wise, Fan had visibly lost ground, her feistiness gone; at least on this blistering night it seemed to be absent. With temperatures during the day well above one hundred degrees, it would be asking the impossible for her to carry his one hundred seventy pounds across the desert. Jerry decided the only chance for them to make it would be for him to walk. Between the realization of what lay ahead and the pesky insects buzzing around him, Jerry slept little. At 2:00 a.m. it was as cool as it would be all day; he gave up trying to sleep. The sun wouldn't be up for another four hours. Jerry led Fan to the river and made sure she drank her fill and then gave her a can of grain. He filled his gallon water container and canvas bag he had bought, and ate his last two eggs.

– 26 –

The Mojave

California Highway Patrolman Magazine, June, 1946
• *Scalpers Sell Promise of 1946 New Car Delivery for up to $300* •
• *Tire Rationing Remains in Force, Supply Lags Demand* •
• *35 MPH War Time Speed Limit Changed to 55MPH* •

Setting a southwest course on his compass, Jerry angled straight across the desert. Following his plan, he walked for four hours at a comfortable stride and then took a fifteen-minute break. Far from Fan's eight-mile-an-hour pace, Jerry figured his was probably more like three, but it was easier on Fan and progress nonetheless. Bright moonlight filtering through the trees, cacti, and bushes cast eerie shadows on a landscape still unseen. Jerry thought about rattlesnakes but refused to worry about them. Just in case, he wrapped Fan's lead rope around his wrist and held it tight in his hand.

Daylight arrived about five-thirty and the sun rose not long after. He dreaded its appearance and, the minute it came up, he understood why. It stung like a hot iron against his shirt and, with bright sun casting away the night, Jerry saw with crystal clarity what lay ahead. The parched landscape stretched into infinity, the sight of it as daunting as the Salt River, the robbers, the mountain lion, and the Texas Panhandle rolled into one. Jerry's first full look made his knees weak. Dotted with prickly plants, the likes of which he had never seen, this place was a world all its own. In the blink of an eye, the sun's rays bleached the desert's vibrant colors to a lifeless monotone, the same merciless sun intent on frying the two of them in Mother Nature's skillet called the Mojave Desert. Even the sky seemed stripped of its color.

The enormity of what he saw did not change the pace or length of Jerry's stride. Instead, it triggered an automatic response to *not* pause, to *not* stop, to keep moving no matter what. He had learned many lessons on this journey and, foremost, was the importance of maintaining forward progress, however small that progress might be. Sticking to that plan they had made it over twelve hundred miles of tough terrain. He figured each step had delivered them closer to their destination, be it to the top of the Continental Divide or the Mogollon Rim. Whether it was a lesson or survival instinct, Jerry didn't know, but he did not hesitate.

A closer look at the ground revealed iron-stained rocks, scattered everywhere on top of the sand, others half-buried. There were concave depressions in the dirt filled with salt or alkali residue, making them appear as shallow dents in an otherwise flat desert floor. Unfriendly bushes with thorns and spikes demanded his constant attention to keep from running into them. Prickly pear, century cacti, creosote bushes, and scraggly mesquite stood like hardy soldiers, as at home in this inhospitable setting as the peach and plum trees were in the fertile soil of his Guthrie orchard. Jerry spotted the distinctive tracks of a sidewinder in the sand.

During his trip preparations, Jerry had learned that air temperatures could reach one hundred twenty degrees during the day and the sand itself as high as one hundred fifty degrees. He distinctly remembered thinking that they would be across the desert before it got this hot. In the safe confines of the Bar R kitchen, it was impossible to envision this kind of heat. Or to fathom that being wrong about it could cost them their lives. He surely couldn't be the only one who had ever miscalculated the desert's ferocity. Had others done the same? And if so, did they make it? Jerry remembered hearing stories about people suffering from heat prostration. Who had told him or when he heard those stories, he couldn't recall. And, he didn't exactly know what the term "prostration" meant, but by noon that first day he began to get an inkling. Skin that burned like it was on fire, feeling light-headed and disorientated, and being thirsty to the core of his being told Jerry he had discovered its meaning in spades.

Fan had tanked up in the Colorado River. Free of his weight and walking at a reasonable pace, she could go an entire day without drinking. Jerry gritted his teeth and vowed to do the same. Desert Center lay forty miles ahead; they had enough water to make it that far. Assuming he had set his compass accurately, they should come within a mile of it. He would tether Fan in a shady place out of sight, and then go in town only long enough to stock up on water and food. Jerry refused to plan any further than that.

Determined to keep moving, he walked through the first day with a fifteen-minute break every four hours. He kept saying aloud that they would be just fine, but it wasn't his words that kept Jerry's fatigue at bay. Looking at what lay ahead and an all-encompassing fear spurred him onward. He willed away fatigue. The minute he felt signs of it, Jerry fought it by picking up the pace. At each stop he gave Fan water from the canvas bag, plus a handful or two of grain, then as soon as she was finished they moved on. He did not remove her saddle; to do so would double the time of each break. As long as they kept moving forward they would be okay.

The sun finally set on their first day. Jerry stopped long enough to eat a can of pork and beans and drink a cup of water. He watered and fed Fan and, for a moment, thought how nice it would be to sleep. But the image of a slithering sidewinder spurred him to resume walking.

His pace had not changed the next morning when daylight arrived. With a total of two hours for breaks out of the previous twenty-eight hours since leaving the Colorado River, Jerry figured they at least had covered forty miles. Since midnight he had kept an eye out for lights off to his left, but saw none. "We should have come right by Desert Center, Fan. What happened?" Jerry scanned the morning horizon to the south—no sign of a town. Only endless desert, endless sky. He was afraid to turn south toward the highway; he couldn't chance running into the highway patrol. Equally fearing to veer from his SW heading and off-course, Jerry kept walking.

Morning flowed into the second afternoon without notice. Jerry willed himself to forget the sun searing from above and the heat boiling up from the sand. He concentrated on keeping a steady pace, counting with an imaginary cadence in his head to keep focused. His step had undoubtedly slowed but the compass remained constant, which meant as long as they kept moving, they would intersect the highway at Indio, the next town.

As the day wore on, it became more difficult to maintain his concentration. His mind kept drifting. Jerry relived the moment that his commander told him his navy career was over; it seemed inconsequential now. He thought about his brothers at home, and his brother Jimmy—maybe in California, maybe in Guam. *Do they miss me? Does Jimmy even know I'm on this trip? Are Mom and Dad worried?* He imagined lavender perfume so clearly, he could smell it and envision pretty Claire Elizabeth Dupree behind the counter of her daddy's store. And dark-haired Sheila, stopping by his table with a salad and a dazzling smile. *That salad tasted so good.*

Jerry wondered if Charles Goodnight had ever been in a predicament like this. *This hot, this thirsty, this alone. What would a great man like that do? What would Grandpa and Frank do?* The miles, the vistas, the people, the hardships and the funny moments mixed and twisted and swirled into a sun-baked montage. Jerry had to keep rousing himself back to the present, to remember what day it was, to check his compass and to look back and make sure Fan was still following. Even though he fought against them, morbid thoughts crept into his mind. *If I had drowned in the Salt River or been shot to death in New Mexico, it would have been over quick. Out here it can be from the heat, or running out of water, or a snake bite—anything could kill me and I'd have plenty of time to see it coming.*

The realization that death could so easily come gave Jerry a jolt.

He tried to pick up his pace but Fan would not. She plodded along with her eyes half-closed, asleep on her feet. Jerry grew fearful that she would just suddenly lie down and give up. Sometime during the night they had finished the water in the canvas bag. His gallon canteen was now all they had. "Keep moving or die…keep moving or die," he muttered in a sing-song voice under his breath.

To keep from drifting off, and make sure he maintained his compass heading, Jerry played a game. Using the sun's position and the length and angle of his shadow, he guessed the time and then checked it against his watch—the goal being to hit it exactly. The game required enough concentration and mental acuity to keep his focus for a few minutes so Jerry upped the ante, trying to guess the beginning of each hour.

That lasted until three o'clock when he began looking for shade. A scraggly mesquite bush about his height was all Jerry could find. He positioned Fan on the shady side of it then knelt in her shadow and poured two cups of water into his hat. Jerry scooped the water over Fan's face again and again, letting it fall back in the hat. Afterward, he washed out the inside of her mouth with his hand. Keeping the tissues of her mouth moist was now more important than getting water into her stomach. An old cowboy who said he'd been in the Foreign Legion in North Africa had told him that, but again Jerry couldn't remember when or where. He drank the water that remained.

Dusk came. Blessed dusk. The sun sank below the horizon at the end of their second day, allowing Jerry's sun-burnt eyes to open instead of squint. Like an alarm clock, the sun's disappearance signaled the desert coming to life. Field mice and lizards scooted out of his way, scorpions and tarantulas scuttled under rocks as he walked by. Jerry heard the sweet sound of birds singing, and wondered where they hid during the day. A black-tailed jack rabbit bounded past, startling him with its energy. Jerry thought of the rabbit he'd eaten with William and Elias, and that reminded him how hungry he felt. He almost stepped on a tortoise that quickly chose to withdraw into the safety of its shell when Jerry brushed it with his boot. The welcome presence of life, however minute or unrelated, lifted his spirits. It offered hope; it stirred him back to reality and forced aside the sun's mind-numbing stupor. Dusk was the best part of the day, when the sky changed to the gold of Oklahoma wheat fields then slid through layers of reds, oranges, and pinks, and finally settled into deep purple and the promise of night.

"We won't miss Indio, Fan. We missed Desert Center, easy to do out here where everything looks the same. It'll be all right, girl, we're going to run right into Indio." Jerry's gallon canteen could last another twenty-four hours if they drank only enough to moisten the tissues of their mouths. Indio was one hundred miles from the Colorado River. *If my heading is true, it can't be more than twenty or thirty more miles. This time I can't afford to miss.*

Jerry walked through his second night and into the third day, cognizant only that they had passed from dark to light. Walking at half the speed of his first day, he didn't know for sure if he slept while he walked, but he suspected he had. Quickly checking his compass heading, Jerry looked back to make sure Fan was still there. The sight of her plodding along, one hoof in front of the other seemingly unaware of the scorching earth, broke his heart. Jerry wondered if hooves burned like human feet, and if hers hurt. He could no longer feel the heat coming through his boots; he couldn't feel his feet at all. Jerry's new size thirty-two Denim Riders, the ones he'd bought in Phoenix, slipped low on his hips. *It's okay, I'll gain it back*, he thought, hitching them up. He avoided saying "if", though the nagging thought remained in the back of his mind. His eyes were scorched and he could feel sores on his dry, cracked lips. His hair had grown long again, matted and stiff with sweat. He hadn't stopped to shave or brush his teeth since leaving the Colorado River. The mirror remained in his pack; he wanted no reminder of how he looked.

Out of the corner of his eye Jerry spied something a few feet off to his right; a pile of bleached bones, maybe a lost steer or mule it looked like. Still in the position in which it died, each bone in place and undisturbed, he envisioned Fan looking that way if she lay down and gave up. Jerry glanced over his shoulder.

Fan's eyes did not open nor did her stride change. He called back to her in a raspy voice. "Do you have any idea how nice it's going to be when we get to Hollywood? It's pretty and green with lots of shade. I promise, Fan, you'll have all the hay and grain and cool water you want. Maybe you'll meet another good-lookin' Appaloosa. And the Pacific Ocean, you've never seen it, Fan. I'll bet you'd like swimming in it. I know I would. I think I'll buy me a bathing suit, and we'll jump in there." He looked back; her eyes didn't open but she flicked her ears.

Hunger drove Jerry to open his last can of beans. Gagging at the taste, he forced himself to eat as he walked. The beans didn't need to be heated; he could hardly hold onto the hot tin can. At dusk, he ate his last can of peaches and gulped down the sweet liquid. They tasted as good as the ice cream in Springerville, but the sweetness only added to his thirst.

They were now out of food except for three slices of bread. Their canteen was less than half full, and they only had a handful of grain left. Jerry had to face the truth. *If we don't come to Indio soon, we're at the end of the line.* Jerry fed Fan the last of her oats. He tore the three slices of bread into pieces and held them in cupped hands toward Fan. The bread disappeared and Fan nudged him for more.

Tears stung at the sight of Fan eating stale bread and wanting more. It hurt more than his own hunger. "Horses shouldn't have to eat dried-out bread, especially you. You shouldn't even be in this God-forsaken place." Jerry rubbed Fan's muzzle; she nuzzled his hand, wanting food. He turned and started walking. "You don't know anything about a bet, or Jimmy Wakely saying cowboyin' is dead. You have no idea that there's a Hollywood up ahead with cool water and plenty of food. You must think I've led you into hell and you're gonna die." Afraid to falter, Jerry didn't turn around. He talked to the desert and hoped that the despair he felt didn't filter through in his voice for Fan to hear. He kept his pace steady but refused to look back. It hurt too much to see what he had done to his horse.

Jerry couldn't stop; he couldn't comfort Fan. He could only put one foot in front of another and wonder. *Could the compass be wrong? Did I somehow miscalculate? Maybe we're nowhere near Indio. God, what if we're walking in circles?* He thought about putting Fan out of her misery or letting her go, but he could not bring himself to do either. An inner voice told him to not give up, that Fan would die without him, and he without her. He looked all around and seeing no one, decided the voice must be his own.

Jerry Van Meter was saying not to give up.

Dark settled over the desert at the end of their third day. *If we don't find Indio, this is it. We won't make it through another day. God, don't let Fan quit, don't let her lay down and give up. I won't leave her. If she stops, it'll be the end of both of us.* With the truth came peace; it was comforting to know that he would not leave Fan, no matter what. After all they had been through he would not leave her to die alone. He owed her that much—either Fan would walk out of this desert with him or he would stay with her until the end.

Jerry's emotional mind told him their situation was hopeless; his rational mind told him he'd set the right compass course and Indio had to be somewhere close. The quarter-moon cast a pale light over the sand. Jerry walked, glancing up at millions of stars then scanning the landscape for lights, for any sign of a city. He told himself that they had to have come at least thirty miles; he should be able to see Indio. Imperceptibly the desert floor changed but it took several minutes for it to register that something was different. Jerry's heart started pounding. His legs trembled and his lungs burned.

What's happening? Am I dying? It suddenly dawned on Jerry that the ground was no longer flat, that he was walking uphill. He looked back; Fan hadn't changed her pace. The climb seemed endless, each step an effort. He had no idea how far or how long it took, but when finally the desert leveled out, Jerry found himself standing atop a knoll and, for the first time since leaving the Colorado River, he could see distance. Off to his right he saw the silhouette of low mountains and more mountains outlined against the sky to the south. And instead of only desert, only sky, Jerry saw a beautiful sight. A cluster of lights twinkled in the distance, a far-off Mecca sparkling with the promise of life.

"That has to be Indio, Fan. If we can see it, we can make it. Come on, girl, let's get out of this desert."

– 27 –

Is That Real Shade or a Mirage?

Indio Press Enterprise, June 15, 1946
• *Indio Remains Hub of Coachella Valley Agricultural Industry* •
• *3/8 Sq Mile Downtown Garners Indio Dubious Distinction as
Smallest City in Country* •
• *Philippine Independence Inaugural Set for July 4 in Manila* •

Jerry wasn't sure whether the buildings in front of him were a product of his sun-baked delirium, or real barns and stables with shade so deep that his sun-burned eyes could not penetrate it. The sun had been up for an hour when he led Fan under the *Riverside County Fairgrounds* sign and into the building it identified. When his eyes adjusted, he could see horses peeking at them from out of their stalls. To make sure he wasn't hallucinating, Jerry touched the nearest wall and took a deep breath. The wood was rough to the touch and the barn smells wonderfully familiar. Only then did Jerry believe they had made it.

A cowboy materialized out of the shade and walked toward them, his look of surprise quickly changing to shock and alarm. "My God, man, did I see right? Did you just walk in off the desert?" Jerry nodded and looked around, not sure what to do first, wanting to savor if only for a moment, their victory over the desert. *Shade. Wonderful, blessed shade.* His eyes came to rest on the fancy-dressed cowboy still staring at them. Jerry's look must have spurred him to action, for the cowboy turned on his heel and ran, immediately returning with a bucket of water. Jerry placed it under Fan's muzzle and she sucked up half of the water in a single drink. He splashed water over her face and let her drink the rest. "Tastes good, huh?" he whispered. His voice sounded strange, totally unlike his own. It hurt to talk. His throat felt like dried jerky; all the water in the world could not make it moist again.

The cowboy sprinted off with the empty bucket and came back in an instant with it full again. This time, Jerry plunged both hands in and splashed water over his head and face, then drank from his cupped hands. Cool and sweet, the water tasted like it had come right out of the well at the Bar R. Fan nudged forward, wanting more. The cowboy held the bucket for her and she drank the rest of the water in one long slow drink.

"Come on," the cowboy said. "You don't need to be standing here. Both of you need help—and fast." Jerry followed silently. Leading them away from the desert entrance to an empty stall in the middle of the large barn, the cowboy opened the stall gate. "Let me get her saddle off for you. You don't look like you have the strength to lift it."

Jerry shook his head. "No, I'll do it," he whispered.

"Well, what can I do? I know something half-dead when I see it."

"My horse needs food, timothy hay if they have it. And rolled oats. Here, I'll get the m…" Jerry started to reach in his pocket.

The cowboy turned and took off in a run. "Don't worry about it," he shouted over his shoulder. "Be right back!"

Fan stood still as Jerry removed her bridle. He unbuckled the cinch and tried to lift the saddle. It didn't budge; it felt ten times heavier than usual. With trembling arms he tried with everything he had to lift it and this time the saddle came off. Jerry hoisted it up onto the top rail of the stall. The saddle blanket came off with it and dropped to the floor. Jerry glanced down at the blanket and spotted the hide stuck to it at the same moment the smell of raw, putrid flesh hit him. Like a hot furnace blast, the stench of foul, decaying tissue exploded in his nostrils, filling the stall. Jerry gagged and gasped for air.

He could only stare dumbfounded. Great patches of skin had come off Fan's back, still attached to the wet saddle blanket. Too stunned to react, Jerry blinked unbelieving and looked again. It was true! Huge raw, bloody sores invaded by pus covered her back. Fan's skin had literally cooked from the moisture and heat under her saddle.

Jerry's head swam. He collapsed down onto his knees, no longer able to stand, unable to speak. Shock, fatigue, and guilt combined to overwhelm him, stomping him in the gut as they raced though his exhausted system, wreaking havoc on his defenseless heart. Tears ran down his cheeks and Jerry covered his face with his hands, silently rocking back and forth on his knees. *I can't take it. I can't take anymore. This is too much. I am killing my horse.*

The squeak of an approaching wheelbarrow echoed through the barn. *The guy with the hay.* Jerry struggled to his feet and was wiping his face with his sleeve when he heard the wheelbarrow stop in front of Fan's stall. The cowboy looked over the gate and, with eyes wide he let out a low whistle. "My God, look at that," he whispered.

Jerry said nothing. There was nothing he could possibly say.

The cowboy glanced at him, his expression betraying instant awareness. "Hey, it'll be okay. I could fetch a vet, but I think if we clean the sores and put some Bag Balm on them, she'll get well on her own. What do you think?"

Jerry shrugged. "I don't know…I'm not sure. I need to get the pus off, but I don't have any disinfectant and I'm out of Bag Balm. I don't know what to—"

"You could use some help, partner. The name's Kevin Lamb, from Idaho." He reached through the stall gate and touched Fan's muzzle. "You could use some help, too."

Jerry nodded. "We must look pitiful. Guess we both could."

Kevin picked up the bucket of water sitting on top of the hay bale and handed it over the rail. "I'll be back as quick as I can with some disinfectant, a can of Bag Balm, everything we need to take care of your horse. You quit worrying and drink some more water. We'll have your mare tended to in no time."

Jerry took a long drink and gave Fan the rest; she emptied the bucket. He stared at her. "Fan, what in God's name have I done to you? We made it, but at what price?"

Fan's demeanor shouted total defeat, her head drooping as low as it would go, tail hanging limp, not making any effort to swish away the flies buzzing around her. Jerry leaned against the wall and closed his eyes against the painful sight. He was still leaning against it twenty minutes later, empty bucket in hand, and sound asleep when Kevin came back.

"Hey, partner, wake up. Let's take care of your horse, then you can get cleaned up and you both can sleep. By the way, what's your name?"

"Jerry," he answered, opening his eyes. It took a moment to realize they weren't in the desert. Exhaustion, hunger, and dehydration had conquered him, just as it had his horse. He blinked and his eyes slowly focused. His body didn't want to move. All defenses were down but Fan needed immediate attention. He nodded at Kevin Lamb, who had changed from his fancy western duds into worn jeans and shirt, and scuffed boots that looked as shabby as his own. The Idaho cowboy had a shock of blond hair and blue eyes that showed kindness and compassion when he looked at Fan.

He led the way to the washing area, turned on the hose, and handed it to Jerry. Jerry let the cool water flow over Fan and they both began cleaning her. Working on opposite sides of the mare, they first soaped off the dirt and dry, crusted sweat. It pained Jerry to look at her back and it hurt even more to gaze on a totally spent horse. She looked half-dead. Fan reached for the stream of water and Jerry held it steady so she could drink.

"Got your favorite hay waiting for you and some oats," he whispered. "You're out of the sun, Fan. There's shade and plenty of water. You can sleep and rest as long as you need to feel good again like you used to." Jerry choked back tears. His heart was breaking; he could hear it in his own voice.

To Jerry's surprise, Kevin was doing his own reassuring. "Fan, huh? Is that your name, pretty lady? You don't look so pretty right now, but you will when we get you all fixed up." He bent down and massaged her legs with soapy rags. "How's that feel? She's going to be fine, Jerry. Her legs are tired, but they don't seem injured. This is one strong horse. She'll come back." Kevin seemed to be reading Jerry's mind.

"Think so? I hope to God she can. Fan is such a great horse. I'd hate to think I..." Jerry looked away and gritted his teeth.

After they had washed her all over, Jerry rinsed away the dirt, sweat, and soap. Fan did none of her usual stretching or shaking after, but she kept seeking the stream of water and drinking. He could feel her skin cool as they began to rub her down.

"She's a strong horse, but I'm surprised she could carry your weight across the desert," Kevin said as he knelt to dry her flank.

"I never rode her. My mistake was not taking her saddle off from the time we left the Colorado River. We never stopped for more than ten or fifteen minutes. I was afraid if we did, I'd fall asleep and never wake up." Jerry shuddered, picturing the pile of bleached bones.

Kevin straightened up and stared at him across Fan's withers. "You mean to tell me you walked across the Mojave Desert? That's a hundred miles!"

Jerry nodded, but said nothing. He kept trying to tell himself that Fan's injuries were temporary, the unfortunate side-effects of the trip, but he knew better. What he had put her through could very well have permanent consequences. *What if she can't come back?* Jerry could not erase the picture of her plodding along behind him through what could only be described as hell on earth. Nor could he forget his thought of putting her out of her misery.

Kevin interrupted his gruesome thoughts. "I ride the rodeo circuit all over the west, calf roping. I've seen horses with sores under their saddles lots of times. They get bunged up just like cowboys. You just have to know what to do and keep doing it," he said.

Fan flinched when Jerry and Kevin cleaned the pus from her

wounds. They patted each raw spot with clean cloths soaked in hydrogen peroxide. Kevin took note of Jerry's stricken look. "Fan's skin's is tender, Jerry, but the peroxide doesn't hurt. I think this is hurting you more than your horse."

With the two of them working, it didn't take long to clean and doctor Fan's sores. Kevin disposed of the pus-covered rags then returned quickly with clean ones to apply Bag Balm on her entire back. Half-way through the application, Fan fell asleep.

"I think it's important to keep flies off these sores," Kevin said. "I've got a rotating fan I carry with me. Air moving across her back ought to keep the flies off and help the sores scab quicker. Keep her more comfortable, too. What do you say?"

"That would help, but can you sleep in this heat without it?" Jerry said.

Kevin stroked Fan's withers. "I'm a softy when it comes to horses. This one is special. I wish I didn't have to be in Los Angeles tomorrow, but you can use the fan until I leave."

Jerry led Fan back to the stall, walking slow as Kevin ran ahead. By the time Fan and Jerry arrived, he had spread a thick layer of fresh straw over the floor. He'd piled her favorite timothy hay in the corner and filled a low round pan with rolled oats. Kevin held up a handful of hay. "Here, Fan, after what you've been through, this is the equine equivalent of a chocolate fudge sundae. Eat up, girl."

The stall still smelled of putrid flesh. Fan's saddle blanket, thrown over the railing, reeked of it. Kevin told Jerry to get his things together for a shower and then disappeared with the blanket. Jerry leaned against the wall, content to see Fan cleaned up and eating. When Kevin came back without the blanket, he addressed Jerry. "I cleaned and hosed it off real good, used a bar of lye on it. It's hanging out back in the sun, which believe me is hot enough to disinfect it. I'll be back in a second with the fan from my room. I'll bring you a clean towel while I'm at it."

He directed Jerry to the small, board-enclosed shower next to the horse washing area. Jerry wrapped himself in his dirty towel and walked with tender feet. The tiny stall had cold water only, but it couldn't have felt any better out of gold faucets at the Ritz Hotel. Jerry stood under the spray and was shaving his face and neck by feel when Kevin returned with a clean towel and the fan.

"This feels so good I hate to get out, but I need food." Jerry brushed his teeth and put on his clean shirt and jeans. Clothes that weren't stiff with sweat felt almost as good as the shower. His mouth tasted clean and his hair smelled of pine-scented soap, but Jerry's feet could not be that easily relieved. The bottoms of both felt like they had been fried on a griddle. Refusing to look, he gritted his teeth, applied a generous layer of Bag Balm, and willed them to get better.

By the time Fan had drunk her fill, all-told she had consumed seven or eight gallons of water. She ate half of the oats and a little of the hay and then abruptly stopped. She lowered herself onto the straw and then laid flat out, the picture of a horse beyond exhaustion. Jerry wiped away tears with the sleeve of his clean shirt.

Kevin gave him a "don't worry, she's going to be alright" look. He secured the oscillating fan to the top rail, faced it down toward Fan's back and turned it on. The fan hummed and clicked as it rotated from side to side, ruffling the loose straw around the sleeping mare. She did not move. Except for her side raising and lowering in rhythm with each breath, Fan looked dead.

"You being a cowboy, I don't mind telling you how much it hurts to see her this way," Jerry said quietly, trying to keep the catch out of his voice. "Thanks for your help. As beat as I am, that would have been tough to do by myself."

Kevin spoke softly, his eyes on Fan. "You're welcome, Jerry. More than welcome. That's one special horse. She's got heart. That's why I know she'll come back. The important thing is that she's taken care of now, watered and fed and sound asleep. The best thing for her, and exactly what you need. You must be starving. Let me scrub up and change my clothes. We can't do anything more for Fan now. Let's go get a bite of breakfast. I'm dying to hear the story that goes with you staggering in off the desert."

– 28 –

The Blue Plate Special

Indio Press-Enterprise, June 15, 1946
• *Indio Population Projected 112,000 by Year 2,000* •
• *Pitchers Feller, Newhouser, & Chandler Tilt Odds to American League in Upcoming All-Star Clash* •
• *Vietnam Uprising Sparks War with France* •

Jerry couldn't help taking note of Indio's tiny downtown, no more than a half-mile long. The 10:00 a.m. sun bounced off deserted sidewalks already reflecting heat waves upward in the still morning air. Singled roofs extended over the walks in front of a few buildings. Good idea, Jerry thought as he took a last look and then followed Kevin into the coffee shop of the New Traveler's Hotel and Café. Indio certainly didn't compare to Springerville, maybe because it was forty degrees hotter.

The waitress led them to a booth directly under a ceiling fan and placed two glasses of water on the table. At the first whiff of food, Jerry's hunger awoke. "I need something more than breakfast." He put the water glass to his lips. "Ouch, these sores hurt."

"The blue plate special is chicken-fried steak and homemade biscuits. All I have to do is mash the potatoes. Would you like that?" the waitress said.

"That sounds good," Jerry said. Kevin ordered the same. A few minutes later when he eyed the sizzling piece of chicken-fried steak and mountain of mashed potatoes covered with cream gravy, Jerry realized the depths of his hunger. "These sores are going to make it tough to eat." He made a concentrated effort to eat slowly. When he finally pushed his plate away, not a morsel remained.

Kevin must have said, "I'll be damned," twenty times during their meal as Jerry told him about the bet between Jimmy Wakely, his grandfather and Frank. He talked at length about the ride, right down to the unfriendly border guard warning him not to sneak across. "But after coming all this way, I wanted to at least set foot in California. We crossed the river about fifteen miles north of Ehrenberg. Have you heard anything about this interdiction?"

"Not a word, but I just drove down from the San Joaquin Valley so I haven't been anywhere near the border. Nobody's been asking questions around the fairgrounds though. Maybe they're just clamping down between here and the state line."

Jerry shook his head. "We wouldn't have come across the desert in the first place if it hadn't been for that. My plan was to stick close to the highway, but I didn't because I was afraid of running into the law. I hate to think Fan and I went through that ordeal for nothing."

Kevin pushed away his empty plate. "Well, I'm sure there is an interdiction. No reason for the guard to lie. If they wouldn't let me across after coming all that way, I'd have done the same thing."

The friendly waitress came by to check. Finding clean plates, she told them they had earned a free dessert. She brought out two dishes of vanilla pudding over sliced bananas on a base of vanilla wafers. And with it, Jerry had his first cup of coffee in over a week. Both cowboys finished off their dessert and Jerry paid for their meals with a five-dollar bill.

"You the cook?" Jerry asked. The waitress nodded hesitantly as she gave him his change. "Then you have to be from Oklahoma. That dessert and the cream gravy could have come right out of my mother's kitchen in Guthrie. And those Okie biscuits couldn't be better."

She beamed. "I am from Oklahoma. Born in Ardmore."

"Well, you are one fine cook," Jerry said. "A great meal."

Kevin thanked Jerry for lunch as they walked back along Highway

111 to Oasis and Arabia Streets and the fairgrounds. They stopped beside his truck and horse-trailer, parked in the shade of the largest building. "I'm leaving early tomorrow, calf-roping in the Gene Autry Rodeo in L.A. I could drive you right to Hollywood. Got an extra stall." He patted his dusty trailer. "Nobody would have to know."

"Thanks, but I would know," Jerry said, not able to ignore the tall, skinny, palm-like trees to the west of the fairgrounds. He hadn't seen them when he stumbled in off the desert. He nodded toward the trees with a questioning look at Kevin.

Kevin turned around. "Date palms." He turned back to Jerry. "Somehow I knew you wouldn't take me up on my offer. By the way, where are you staying in Hollywood?"

"Haven't figured that out yet. I want to meet up with Wakely if he's at his ranch. I'm not sure he's even in Hollywood. He might be away on a singing tour. Exactly what are dates?"

Kevin led the way back into the barn, Jerry following. "They're sort of like a prune, only sweeter and not as wrinkled. You mean to tell me you started out for Hollywood and don't have a place to stay when you get there?" Kevin's incredulous expression matched his voice.

They arrived at Fan's stall and both looked over the rail. She hadn't moved. "That's about the size of it," Jerry said quietly. "Think I'll try me some of those dates. I've never even heard of them."

Kevin chuckled and shook his head. "You Oklahoma cowboys are tough, but crazy. One of my best friends lives in Hollywood. Go to his place. I know he will put you up. His name is Pete Wilson, head stunt man for Republic Pictures. Pete's got twenty acres in North Hollywood where he trains his trick horses. We used to ride rodeos together. Now he only rides if there is one near his home. I never had the brains to get out."

"Exactly what does he do?"

"He takes the fall for the star, like John Wayne. He's done it for Hoot Gibson and Hopalong Cassidy when they were Republic stars. When a horse supposedly gets shot out from under the star and sends

him ass over tea kettle, you can bet it isn't Jimmy Wakely or Roy
Rogers rolling in the dust, or their fancy horse either. If it's a Republic
movie, it's Pete and one of his horses. He's been doing it for fifteen
years."

"I could have used a stunt man on this trip." Jerry said.

"Hell, Oklahoma, you could *be* a stunt man. You sure got the
experience." Kevin wrote down Pete Wilson's address and a brief note
to him and then gave Jerry general directions. "Sorry I can't be more
exact, but not all the streets around his place have names. Anyway,
give this note to Pete and I'll stop by his place before I head out of Los
Angeles. I wish you'd come with me. Make it easy on yourself and
that horse of yours. Fan's going to get better, but it's still another
hundred and fifty miles to Hollywood, and plenty hot."

"Thank you. It's tempting, but I can't. I've come too far to cheat
and I'm not going to ride her for a while yet. I've got an idea to fix the
blanket so nothing touches her back."

"Well, I wish you and Fan the best of luck. You're one helluva
cowboy, Oklahoma," Kevin said. They shook hands.

"Thanks again for all the help. You ain't bad yourself, Idaho. I
hope we meet again."

"I do, too. I'll get my fan after I load up my horses in the morning.
By the time you wake up, I'll be half-way to L.A." They spoke quietly,
both observing Fan as they talked. The cowboy from Idaho with the
kind blue eyes gave a silent wave and disappeared. It was almost noon
when Jerry finally spread his bedroll along the wall in Fan's stall and
took off his boots. His body ached with an all-encompassing weariness, and sleep beckoned with a power he could no longer fight. Jerry
lay down, feeling himself losing consciousness, aware only of the
fan's rhythmic swooshing and its air moving across him. His skin
wasn't on fire; he wasn't dirty and hungry anymore. And most
important, he and Fan still had a chance. He said a brief prayer of
thanks, glanced at his sleeping horse and then closed his eyes. It had
been eighty-two hours since he awoke at two a.m. at the Colorado

River, unable to sleep because of pesky insects and the daunting journey ahead.

Jerry accomplished a great deal in the two days he spent in Indio. He fashioned Fan's clean saddle blanket into a protective cover that allowed nothing to touch her healing skin. Folding the blanket into several thicknesses, he cut holes in it the exact size of her sores. The thick blanket layers now rested on healthy skin and left an air space over the scabbing sores where neither blanket nor saddle could touch.

He trimmed her hooves and put on new rock shoes. Like the worn-out ones he replaced, they were made of solid iron and rimmed with a one inch lip to make them last longer. Evidently they weren't designed for crossing the Mojave Desert, for Jerry was able to bend her old rock shoes with his fingers; they were paper thin.

He groomed Fan several times a day and fed her sweet, ripe apples for treats. He replenished his food supplies—no pork and beans on the list. He hoped he would never have to eat them again. Jerry bought a bag of dates and ate them like candy. He wrote a letter to his parents and brothers, also one to Rolla and Frank. When he thought about trying to tell them about crossing the desert, Jerry decided no words could describe the experience, so he wrote that he didn't much care for it. And he slept. The moment he lay down on his bedroll, Jerry fell into a deep sleep. Fan did the same—on her feet after the first day. Except for a twenty-minute walk through the shady complex of open barns twice a day to help her keep limber, Fan spent her time in Indio either eating, drinking, or sleeping. Jerry watched her come back to life like a wilted flower after being watered. Their last evening in the tiny desert city brought a treat.

A freak Pacific storm roared up through the Gulf of California, bringing with it cooler air, lightning, thunder, and rain. The storm lingered for the whole evening before it blew out over the desert. The arrival of rain brought out the Indio residents Jerry had yet to see, all of them enjoying *the gift* as they called it.

He left Indio at dawn the following morning by the same means he arrived—on foot and leading his horse. It was day forty-five, and they had one hundred forty miles to go. "Fan, we're gonna be in Hollywood by day fifty, come hell or high water. We've been through both and neither one has stopped us."

– 29 –

The Place That God Forgot

California Highway Patrolman Magazine, June, 1946
• *California Celebrates 50 Year Anniversary of First Motor Car* •
• *Freight Shipments, Passenger Travel to Europe and South America
Expected to Increase Air Travel by 50%* •
• *40M Aircraft, Auto and Ordnance Parts Built in 1,249 Days of War* •

A leaner, more determined Jerry Van Meter walked out of Indio before daylight on June 17, 1946. He began the last leg of his journey feeling he could look Rolla and Frank in the eye, man to man, and no longer hang his head about anything.

Leading Fan west alongside the railroad tracks, he passed rows of long, metal-roofed packing sheds already humming with activity. Though it was still dark, not far beyond the sheds was a large area that appeared to be a shanty town; tiny shacks with people sleeping outside, others beginning to stir. Campfires glowed in front of the shacks with women moving about, bending low over their fires tending to pots that filled the rain-freshened air with the inviting aroma of food— a reminder of Cibecue.

Only there was no Indian rodeo here, and these fires weren't intended to feed Apache onlookers in a festive mood. They were to feed hundreds of Mexican workers who helped to produce and harvest the agricultural riches of the Coachella Valley. Jerry and Fan passed fields of row crops, unidentifiable in the dark, and then acres of tall date palms, their thin trunks and pom-pom tops poking fifty and sixty feet into the sky. He wondered how in the world workers harvested dates.

Despite what he'd heard from Kevin about the interdiction, Jerry did not want to chance running into a patrolman, or anyone who might know about it and summon the authorities. The vast expanse of desert on the north side of Highway 10 belonged to the federal government. He had asked the waitress at the coffee shop about it. No development and no people, it would be a mile or two out of the way, but worth it. They crossed the darkened highway and walked north and then west. When he could no longer see lights or hear cars, Jerry corrected their course to due west.

They were again in the wide-open desert, though it looked a bit different than the landscape they encountered near Indio. Not flat and endless, but desert nonetheless, with a bright moon glistening off light sand and sparse vegetation specialized to survive in arid climates. Jerry noticed a new shape he hadn't seen before; tall silhouettes that looked like trees, but with prickly limbs like a cactus. He busied himself noting bushes and shadowy shapes, making sure he weaved around them to avoid rattlesnakes.

This part of the desert did not fill Jerry with the same level of dread and fear he experienced that morning with his first sight of the Mojave. He had conquered it before; he could do so again. But his surroundings did reintroduce an element of vigilance, the sand, the eerie shapes and heat recreating a similar feeling in Jerry's gut. Thankfully, completely gone was the despair he experienced moments before he spotted Indio's distant lights when he realized he and Fan would not last another day. Fear conquered, nevertheless Jerry glanced back at Fan to make sure she was alright. Her head up and alert look brought assurance and a smile.

"How you doing back there, Fan?" Her ears flicked back and forth and she nickered softly. "Well, I'll be damned, you actually answered." He admitted her gait couldn't be called lively, but it was definitely better. Jerry felt the same way. His step betrayed a new-found confidence. No longer an unknown, he knew the desert for what it was: one more enemy in a long line of enemies. It differed only from a raging river or a Rocky Mountain snow storm, or from men wanting to kill him in that this enemy used unforgiving, never-ending heat. Jerry's original plan to follow Highway 10 across the desert had been a good plan, well thought-out but with one critically important hitch—an unforeseen law and an officious border guard that nearly cost them their lives. While relating the story to Kevin, it occurred to Jerry that his fear of Fan being impounded, combined with his fatigue and the endless mind-numbing heat, had adversely influenced his judgment. Leaving the safety of the highway was a crucial decision—an almost fatal one. He would not make the same mistake again. Jerry made a silent promise to stay out of the law's reach, but this time within reasonable limits.

The sun came up, dissipating any lingering freshness from the previous night's rainstorm and bringing with it blinding glare and blistering heat. The unfamiliar shapes Jerry had spotted turned out to be Joshua trees, tall thorny-branched brothers of the yucca plant. They cast meager but welcome shade. This part of the Mojave Desert with its low, rolling hills appeared different from the desert east of Indio. Looking north, its contour reminded Jerry of the gently rolling hills of Oklahoma, except it was covered with sand instead of crops. But he had learned something about this part of the Mojave. It was no ordinary desert; it had a story.

According to the waitress at the New Traveler's Hotel coffee shop, this part of the Mojave had been home to one of America's biggest war heroes. During last night's dinner, she told the story in segments on her intermittent stops at his table. General George Patton and his wife, Beatrice, had been Indio residents for a brief time during the war. She said that young George Patton had grown up in this part of California, then decades later as General, felt that the Mojave Desert was not just similar to the North African desert, it was worse.

Because of Patton's familiarity with the Mojave, the War Department picked him to establish and command the Desert Training Center (DTC) in the early months of 1942. Overnight, the army invaded the area, bringing in hundreds of soldiers, trucks, and equipment. Airplanes flew in and out of the hastily built runway with important Washington brass on board. Cargo planes delivered tons of supplies and armored tanks and flat-tracks could be seen being unloaded off railcars near Desert Center. Within a few months, the two thousand residents of Indio and the rest of Coachella Valley found themselves smack in the middle of the war.

For a few days before he moved his base camp twenty miles east of Indio, General Patton and his staff had used the New Traveler's Hotel as their headquarters. The waitress said the general's booming voice could be heard "from one end of town to the other." That reminded Jerry of Rolla and Frank's stories about Charlie Goodnight's blistering language and bellowing voice. Jerry had to smile at the thought that he and Fan had walked through the very same desert where General Patton chose to train troops and tank commandos in survival and desert warfare.

The waitress said that the first troops to arrive at the Desert Training Center had called it "the place that God forgot." Jerry instinctively knew what that meant. "Hey, Fan. Since we beat this desert, think we can survive most anything?" Jerry looked back at her, confident that no greater truth could be said. All told, over two million DTC troops and tank officers commanded by General Patton, had survived training exercises in this ten thousand square miles of Mojave Desert. And it was the same personnel and equipment of the Second Corps that helped Patton defeat the Germans in the deserts of North Africa, and later in Sicily. The image of the general reinforced Jerry's confidence.

He walked for three hours and then stopped for a thirty-minute rest. This time he removed Fan's saddle and turned it on its side in the shade, the hot air drying moisture on her back and dampness in the saddle blanket. A time-consuming process but it worked; the scabs remained intact. It also ate up precious ticks of the clock.

Remembering how Fan had responded to his and Kevin's voice, Jerry sang as he walked, as many cowboy songs as he could recall. When he ran out of songs, Jerry talked. "You realize, don't you, that you're helping Grandpa win a bet for cowboys everywhere? You've already proved that horses today are as tough as they ever were. Hell, you're tougher than any horse I ever heard of." He talked about the pretty sights they had seen and the people they met. He figured that Fan wouldn't know *what* he was saying, but she would know by the tone of his voice that this time it held no despair.

The heat was as unmerciful and the sun equally blinding, but on this day Jerry did not have trouble concentrating. He harbored no thought of letting Fan go or that they might not make it. The difference had little to do with occasional shade or proximity to a highway. The desert that tried to kill him was no longer a great unknown. Jerry knew its limits and now he knew his own.

At four o'clock, he adjusted the angle of his path to a more southerly direction and half an hour later, Highway 10 came back into view. As they approached its edge, Jerry scanned the stretch of asphalt in both directions for black and white Packards but thankfully saw none. He led Fan across the highway, back over the railroad tracks, and headed into the eastern outskirts of Palm Springs.

– 30 –

The Long Arm of the Law

The Desert Sun, June 18, 1946
• *Meat Shortage? Lots of Beef but it's all on the Hoof* •
• *Four Lanes for Palm Canyon Drive-Lights to Replace Stop Signs* •
• *Directors Edgar Bergen, Leonard Firestone form Corporation*
to Develop Former DTC Tank Repair Facility •

"We could have bummed a ride on the train in Indio and saved ourselves walking all day, not to mention some sore, hot feet. You ever been on a train, Fan?" Jerry looked back, expecting to see a lethargic horse plodding along. Instead she had speeded up and there was a determination in her step. Ten minutes later he found out why. A river running along the border of a huge orange grove lay directly in their path.

Fan walked down the bank into the water and immediately started to drink. She kept one eye and ear trained on Jerry, the other scanning the orchard to her right. On closer inspection, the river looked more like a canal; the water ran slow but was deep enough that it reached the underside of Fan's belly. Jerry sat on the grass-covered bank eyeing the orange orchard while she drank. He could hardly wait to enter its inviting shade.

Looking toward the west, the orchard looked to be an endless mass of green trees disappearing in the distance. Five o'clock, the hottest hour of the day, the sun's fiery rays snaked beneath Jerry's hat brim searing his eyes and rendering his Stetson useless. He considered removing his boots and joining Fan until he noticed her looking

197

around like she was about to lie down in the water. Jerry didn't have time to remove his boots before reacting; he jumped in and grabbed an apple from his saddle bag. Only then did Fan willingly follow him out of the canal and into the deep shade of the orange grove.

"Fan, you would have gotten everything wet!" Jerry's new jeans were soaked up to his pockets and, with each step his boots squished water over the tops. "How can I get upset with you? At least my legs are cool."

Jerry hurriedly switched Fan from bridle to halter and tethered her to a tree; she wanted the apple he promised. Her expectant happy-face expression greeted his outstretched hand full of apple slices. "You and your treats, I wish I had one of those strawberry ice cream cones about now." Removing her saddle, Jerry was pleased to see the scabs intact and no sign of pus.

The orchard had recently been irrigated. Wide furrows ran down the center of each row. The earth at the bottom of the furrow was muddy but only damp on the top and under the tree. Jerry walked to the opposite border of the orchard, all the way to a two-lane road. On the other side of the asphalt were more trees; he watched as a group of Mexican workers came out of the orchard. They glanced his way as they loaded their ladders into pickup trucks. Instinctively, Jerry stepped back into the trees.

He discovered the source of the irrigation water, a concrete standpipe at the end of the row. Reaching down inside the pipe, he turned on the valve and the water level quickly rose and then bubbled up and over the sides. After he washed his face and drank from his cupped hands, Jerry turned off the valve and walked back through the trees to Fan. "I know where you can get a drink of water later." He had never been in an orange orchard before. *Mature trees, judging by their height and size of the trunks,* Jerry thought. And despite the heat and the blinding sun a few hundred yards away, deep in the orchard it felt cool. The air smelled sweet and, with a turn of a valve, water bubbled up on demand. Jerry reasoned that if the Mojave represented hell on earth, this orchard represented heaven. Fan ate a bigger-than-usual portion of oats. Jerry ate a peanut butter sandwich, food with no other purpose than to keep him alive.

As soon as he stretched out on his bedroll under a tree, Jerry's weariness returned. More than simple fatigue, it was exhaustion and an acceptance that his body could go no farther this day. It wasn't pain, but heavy limbs, heavy eyes, a rapturous calm that started at his feet and moved upward through his body to the end of his fingers, laced loosely across his chest. Jerry closed his eyes and let himself be enveloped by the coolness, the fragrance, and the absence of the blinding sun.

"I know you're every bit as tired as I am, Fan. Better lay down while you got a shady soft spot to do it," he said quietly. From the sound of her steady breathing, Fan was already asleep.

In the fog of deep sleep, Jerry felt something touch the bottom of his foot. The touch was not enough to rouse him from his trance-like state, but when it came again a little harder, and with a steady tap, tap, tap, his eyes flew open. He was looking straight into the blinding beam of a flashlight. "What the h—?" He tried to sit up, but pressure on his chest pushed him back to the ground. For a frightening moment, Jerry could not remember where he was.

"What do we have here, a vagrant?" The owner of the voice must have already spotted Fan. "I've never seen a vagrant with a horse." The beam moved off Jerry's face. "Sit up, mister, nice and slow."

Jerry sat up, blinking and trying to focus. From his vantage point, he could only see the sharp crease of a pant leg about knee level. Jerry's eyes followed the crease down to the top of a shiny black shoe. *Oh my God, the Highway Patrol.* "I'm not a vagrant," he said, sick with dread, his heart hammering. "Is it okay if I stand up?"

"You carrying a weapon?" The official-sounding voice wanted to know.

"Yes, sir, holster's hanging on a limb above by my saddle."

"Go ahead, stand up, but no sudden moves," the patrolman said with pure authority.

Once upright and on his feet, Jerry's tired muscles signaled he hadn't been asleep very long. He raised his hands, squinting against the beam. The officer moved the light away from his face and Jerry stared directly into the eyes of a California Highway Patrolman about his dad's age. Black hair showed from under a soft-billed cap, but his curious eyes did not match the sternness in his voice. He held a night stick in his right hand.

In the dim light Jerry saw that he dressed exactly like the officers at the border, in a hip length jacket, a wide belt lined with bullets, and a holster with a revolver. He had a seven-point badge pinned on the left side of his jacket, but in the darkness Jerry couldn't make out the writing. "I can explain what I'm doing here. I look bad, but I'm not a bum." *God, I pray he doesn't know about the interdiction.*

"Let's have a look at the weapon." The officer lifted the six-shooter from Jerry's holster. "Hmmh, notches." Spinning the cylinder, he methodically ejected each bullet into his hand and dropped them into his coat pocket. "Got any identification?" He returned the empty Colt to the holster.

"Yes, sir." Jerry lowered his right hand and reached into his hip pocket. No wallet! Fear turned to panic before he remembered that he'd put his wallet in the waterproof tin in his saddle bags. Would you like me to get it?" *I don't have a choice. I have to tell him the truth.*

"Absolutely."

Fan had awakened, frightened by the strange voice and light. Alert, she tossed her head and whinnied. "It's okay, girl." Jerry patted her neck then got on his knees to look through his saddle bags. "Look, officer, me 'n my mare have traveled over a thousand miles. I'm not up to anything bad. I can prove who I am. My name is Jerry Van Meter, from Oklahoma. We're on our way to Hollywood."

"Where in Oklahoma?" The voice sounded a little friendlier.

"Guthrie, it's just north of Oklahoma City."

"I know where Guthrie is. We don't get many gun-toting cowboys around here. When somebody sees one camping out on private property, they get a little nervous. Let's see that ID." The officer shined the flashlight beam over Jerry's shoulder as he went through the tin box that held his papers. The calendar lay on top; he held it up for the officer. "You can see I've marked off every day we've been on the road." He kept digging until he found his wallet at the bottom of the tin. "I keep it in here. We've had to cross a couple of rivers." Jerry pulled out his Oklahoma driver's license and naval identification card and handed them to the officer.

"You can stand up and tend to your horse. I must be making her nervous." Jerry got to his feet and put his hand on Fan's withers, mouthing a silent prayer that the interdiction had been lifted, or if it hadn't, this patrolman didn't know about it. "Navy, huh?" the officer said. He read softly to himself from each card. "Okay, Jerry Van Meter from Guthrie, Oklahoma, what are you doing packing a Colt with notches in the handle and sleeping on private property in Palm Springs, California?"

"Where I live and in my business, it's common to wear a holster and pistol." That prompted the patrolman to ask what Jerry's business was. "I'm a cowboy, foreman on my granddad's ranch near Enid, Oklahoma. We all wear guns. The reason I'm in Palm Springs has to do with a bet my grandfather made with a friend of his, a movie star named Jimmy Wakely."

The officer instantly relaxed his stance then slipped the leather loop of his night stick over a tree limb. "Any self-respecting western fan, which I happen to be, knows who Jimmy Wakely is. Okay, you've got my attention. Explain." He sounded completely friendly now.

Jerry went through the story again, emphasizing the long-standing relationship between his grandfather and Jimmy Wakely. When he finished with the part about his walking across the Mojave, the officer gave a low whistle. "That's the damnedest story I've ever heard." His looked at Jerry with a mixture of admiration and incredulity. "So you rode *this* horse," he pointed to Fan, "all the way from Guthrie to the Colorado River. But why did you walk the rest of the way?" He handed Jerry back his identification.

"I was afraid that with the heat and carrying my weight, my horse wouldn't make it. She still got messed up. You should see her back." Jerry held his breath. *If he knows, this is when he'll hit me with the impound.*

The officer pointed the flashlight beam toward Fan, the scabs readily visible. "I see what you mean." He shoved his cap back and rubbed his forehead. "That's too crazy a story to be a lie, no wonder you look so—"

Jerry exhaled with a chuckle. "I look good compared to what I looked like when we walked in off the desert. We call it trail-dirty and saddle-weary. I haven't had a haircut since Springerville, Arizona. I know I look awful, but I'm so tired there's not much I can do about it."

"I can't imagine anybody walking across the Mojave Desert in this heat and surviving. But you—you look like you did it." He kept shaking his head in disbelief. "Where are you going once you get to Hollywood?" Jerry handed him the note Kevin wrote to the Republic Pictures stuntman. "I'm from Oklahoma," the patrolman said. "My wife and I live over in Hemet now, lots of Okies there. The theater in Hemet plays more westerns than anything else." He rattled off the names of Gene Autry and Roy Rogers movies that Jerry had never heard of. "My wife and I have probably seen every one of Jimmy Wakely's pictures. I bet not more than a month ago we saw him in *Moon Over Montana*. He starred in that one." The officer cupped his chin, the flashlight in his other hand pointing straight down. "And I'm trying to remember, I'm pretty sure I've heard the name Pistol Pete before."

"Pretty famous, actually," Jerry said. "His real name is Frank Eaton. He's the one who put the notches in my Colt, long before I—"

"Wait a minute," he interrupted. "Now I remember. Handlebar

mustache, big ten gallon hat, wears his hair in braids? Isn't his likeness the mascot for Oklahoma A & M?"

"That's him. He'll be pleased you knew that."

"We still go back to Oklahoma City once in a while, lots of family there. Won't they get a kick when I tell them about running into you. It's been a pleasure meeting a real cowboy from my home state. I'll give you a little advice, though. I suggest you put the Colt in your saddle bag for the rest of your trip. Probably save you a lot of explaining."

"I'll do that."

The patrolman retrieved the bullets from his pocket and handed them to Jerry. "Sorry about waking you up. Some field workers called in that they'd seen a bum in here. Hope I didn't scare you half to death."

"That's okay. I understand we're on private property. It's just that when we got to town we were so tired and hot, this orchard practically called our names. My horse headed for the shade like she usually does toward water."

The patrolman chuckled. "Still can't imagine anybody walking across the Mojave Desert. Sounds to me like you've already had considerable good luck, cowboy, but I'll wish more for you anyway. I hope you win the bet." He retrieved his night stick.

"Thanks, I'm going to give it my best."

Jerry watched the flashlight beam disappear into the deepening darkness. When he could no longer see it, he took his first deep breath. "Close, Fan. I thought sure he was going to run us in." Jerry lit a match and checked the time. "Nine o'clock. No wonder I'm still tired. Think you can go back to sleep, Fan?" He heard Fan's steady breathing. "Guess so." Jerry lay back down on his bedroll.

The air felt cool. He could see tiny patches of stars through the trees. *I'm starving, I'll never get back to sleep.* With his last waking thoughts about pie and ice cream, the fragrant air and soft earth lulled Jerry back to sleep as soon as he closed his eyes.

– 31 –

Welcome to the Future

The Desert Sun, June 19, 1946
• *War Assets Corp. Delays Return of City Hospital-Red Tape* •
• *Coloured Thief Offered 30 Day Sentence Reduction to Leave Town* •
• *Phenomenal Growth Predicted for Palm Springs* •

The following morning, Jerry led Fan west onto Palm Canyon Drive and stopped at a restaurant with a bright neon sign beckoning *Open 24 Hours.* He followed his breakfast of ham and eggs and french-fried potatoes, with several cups of coffee and then apple pie and ice cream.

Palm Spring's main street bristled with activity and new development. Buildings stood too far back from the road for him to see, but what he could see bore no resemblance to the arid, desolate land east of Indio or the shanty town on the western outskirts of it. Palm-lined drives curved through spacious grounds carpeted by expansive lawns adorned with elaborate fountains and waterfalls that sparkled in the early morning sun.

He passed a sign pointing down a side street to Troy Roger's *Mink and Manure Club,* heralding it as Palm Spring's newest western nightspot. *Entertainment by Singer Patty Page, Direct from Hollywood.* "I ought to stop in and see what California cowboys look like, Fan." He didn't have to go looking because Jerry encountered more horsemen along Palm Canyon Drive than at any time on the trip. They weren't cowboys; they were members of riding clubs. They all stopped him and introduced themselves as being from this or that "stable." One

205

rider, on a beautifully groomed Palomino, asked Jerry outright why he was leading his horse. Was she injured, did they need help? He offered to accompany them to his riding club nearby. *Friendly people, these Californians,* Jerry thought.

Palm Springs dazzled as much from growth as it did from sunny weather. There seemed to be new construction everywhere he looked. Jerry spotted a massive building in *Thunderbird Ranch*, a huge commercial site being developed. On closer inspection, it turned out to be a high school slated for opening in September 1947. Farther on, another partially-completed structure labeled *Future Home of Bullocks Department Store*, occupied a sprawling site of unfinished commercial buildings. Signs pointed the way to *Tom O'Donnell's Golf Course* and *Charlie Farrell's Racquet Club and Tennis Ranch*. Jerry smiled. *I wonder exactly what they raise on a tennis ranch.* Flags and an elaborate sign marked the entrance to *Tahquitz River Estates,* a series of neat rows of houses laid out on wide streets, some of them framed, others in varying stages of completion. *Palm Springs' Best New Subdivision. Homes from $5,600.*

Contrary to what he had read and heard, Jerry saw no evidence of a building material shortage. Workers scurried about carrying two-by-fours, bricks, and lengths of pipe while construction sounds filled the air. And it seemed that every carpenter, plumber, and roofer drove a pickup truck—more pickups than Jerry had ever seen in one place. This was the progress Jimmy Wakely had tried to explain to Rolla and Frank, "explosive growth, the reawakening of our country." Wakely described it right when he called it "a post-war boom, and the end of an era that would never return."

Not more than forty miles east of Palm Springs, Jerry had left the desert that "used to be." Now in the midst of this city, everywhere he turned he saw a glimpse of what it was "going to be." Phoenix was the same, city boundaries stretching in all directions, full of energy and promise. The future: buildings springing up everywhere; roads being built; developments with signs announcing, "New shopping center with acres of parking" where farmland and orchards had been before. Like crossing the Mojave Desert, Jerry realized that he could not possibly capture all of this in a letter.

On the western outskirts of Banning, twenty miles west of Palm Springs, Jerry decided to ride Fan again. The smaller scabs had come off and the larger ones remained intact. The blanket with holes cut to match her sores had worked as he planned. Now it would have to work with his weight on the saddle. Foot sore and weary to the bone, Jerry had walked more than one hundred thirty-five miles, and he could walk no farther.

It was Wednesday, June 19, day 47; if they did not arrive in Hollywood by Saturday, they would lose the bet. Hollywood lay eighty miles northwest as the crow flies, but they could neither fly like a crow nor travel in a straight line. They had traffic and people to contend with; he would need time to find Pete Wilson's place. Jerry either had to ride Fan or lose the bet. After last night's encounter with the Highway Patrol, the law no longer seemed to be a threat.

Jerry rode alongside Highway 10, the quickest, most direct route into Los Angeles. Fan paid no attention to cars whizzing by at fifty-five miles an hour, or occasional horns. He had grown to love Fan, her nerve, her heart and endless loyalty, her acceptance of whatever life threw her way. It did not go unnoticed that those traits personified the man who gave her to him.

Up ahead, Jerry spied three red and white Burma Shave signs. They called up instant memories of growing up during the Depression. With gas shortages and little money, the Van Meter family rarely took car trips. But when they did, Jimmy, Jerry, Billy, David, and Byron had an understanding that whoever spied the signs first got to read them aloud to the family.

Jerry guided Fan closer. *Are your whiskers when you wake. Tougher than a two-bit steak? Try Burma Shave.*

He rubbed his stubble-covered face and steered Fan back away from the road's edge. Reciting the rhyme under his breath, he remembered rare long-ago drives with his parents and brothers to visit their grandfather at the Bar R. Five boys crammed into the back seat of a 1931 Touring Studebaker and having to sit still for over an hour—which seemed like an eternity. The Studebaker barely coming to a stop at the ranch, they burst out of the car like coiled springs and raced to Grandpa's barns to play. Jerry's smile deepened at the thought. He rode past more citrus groves in Cherry Valley, Calimesa, and Redlands, each town a step farther from the desert.

At the western outskirts of San Bernardino, Jerry turned west and joined the last fifty miles of Route 66, the highway that wound through the hearts of cities, transporting people, commerce, and ideas, creating a fantasy about road travel like no other highway before. Young couples spent their honeymoons traveling the *Mother Road*. Starting in Chicago, it raced westward and ended only when it ran out of real estate in Santa Monica at the ocean's edge.

Tired and dirty, Jerry welcomed the sight of it, like coming across an old friend. He thought back to the Oklahoma prairie and the night he first camped beside the *Mother Road*. Listening to the whine of diesel rigs, watching car lights race by in the fading light, and wondering what adventures awaited him. Although separated for what seemed like a lifetime, here it was again; palm-lined and pointing the way just like he'd dreamed. Hollywood—the end of the journey, a covenant kept, a bet won.

On the north side of Route 66, an arch made from full debarked logs marked the entrance to the *San Gabriel Riding Club*. Jerry headed Fan under the arch into the club's spacious grounds. New buildings and immaculate grounds labeled it a recently completed facility, its wooden fences painted crisp white. Straight rows of corrals, each one filled with groomed horses, formed avenues to the right of the driveway. Stable boys rushed back and forth carrying halters, saddles, and bridles. Riders dressed in riding britches, tall slender boots, formal-looking jackets, and small black hats, stared with open mouths at Jerry and Fan as they rode in. Jerry noted that the stable boys dressed like cowboys—albeit clean-clothed, rested cowboys. He dismounted and led Fan past a bulletin board showing times for riding lessons and classes with names like *Show Techniques* and *Basic Horsemanship.*

He asked a stable boy if they had a place where he and Fan could stay for the night.. "Sure, building number ten to your left. Take any one of those open stalls." His eyes flicked over Fan. "You can give your horse a bath if you want." Covered with dirt and sweat, Fan looked rangy and bedraggled compared to the fancy resident horses. She had lost significant weight; it showed in her girth and withers. Her breast no longer had that layer of fat and muscle that made him tease her about how much she ate. And Jerry could no longer ignore the fact that some of Fan's spirit had disappeared. It gave him a sick feeling and an ache in his chest to see how exhausted and dispirited she looked.

Jerry found the bathing area and washed her off with cool water, then brushed and combed her. He talked as he groomed her, hoping that his voice would perk her up. It had always rallied her before but now seemed to have no effect. Fan ate some hay and rolled oats but her demeanor and appearance screamed of an underlying fatigue that food and loving words could not touch. Once she finished eating, she lowered herself onto the fresh straw, heaved a sigh and put her head down. Sometimes she seemed more like a dog than a horse. Like Toby, the shepherd back at the Bar R, her sigh told Jerry that she considered her job done for the day.

The largest scab remained intact but it had begun to loosen around the edges. Riding Fan from Banning hadn't disturbed it, yet Jerry regretted having to ride her at all. As he watched her sleep, a part of him wished he had taken Kevin up on his offer. Still, the mental image of getting out of Kevin's pickup at Pete's ranch and unloading Fan from the trailer, Jerry knew deep down he made the right decision; he could never cheat.

Fan and Jerry experienced a weariness that could not be remedied with a hearty meal, a cool bath, or a good night's sleep. Enduring heat that never let up, traveling day-in and day-out as many miles as their bodies could withstand, had caused both to dig deep into their reserves. It called on muscle and nerve that had no more to give, yet give more they would have to do.

The Colorado River represented more than the border between two states. It symbolized the line that separated men from boys, and tough horses from pretty horses. And the Mojave Desert embodied the place where a man either conquered or was defeated by his worst fears.

Jerry gazed down at his sleeping horse. "We're almost there, girl, hang on for a little while longer."

– 32 –

Rose Bowl Grass Tastes Better

Los Angeles Times, June 20, 1946
• Head of Paramount's $1.1 Million Salary Highest in Nation •
• Soviet Move to Yugoslav Border Puts U.S. Army on Alert •
• Friends of Generals and Colonels By-Pass War Assets Administration Freeze,
Purchase Surplus Planes •

When Jerry awoke, Fan was standing up munching on hay she hadn't finished the night before. "You're up and you look a little better." She did look better. He did, too. He'd used the shower, then shaved and put on his faded set of clean clothes. His hair had grown down to his collar again. He combed it back and quickly put his Stetson on to keep it in place.

Jerry and Fan rode under the arch onto Foothill Boulevard just as the sun came up. They headed due west, riding along the front of orange grove properties. Orchards lined both sides of the wide boulevard, the trees interrupted occasionally by houses with fenced pastures in front. The farther west they rode, the fewer groves they encountered. Former orchards now sported business or apartment complexes, forcing Jerry and Fan to ride dangerously close to cars racing by. By mid-afternoon he felt spent and Fan's slow pace told him she felt the same way.

It's too early to be this tired, Jerry reminded himself. But fatigue never fully replenished added to the previous day, and the day before that, combining with all the days of the journey like rainwater collecting in a barrel. Increasing in insidious increments, Jerry's and

Fan's exhaustion now threatened to overwhelm the vessel. Early evening found them thirty miles west of San Bernardino in the small town of San Dimas. The minute he spotted *Buddy's Burgers*, Jerry gratefully patted Fan's neck and reined her to a stop. Neon flashed *Hamburgers, Fries, Fresh-Squeezed Orange Juice*. He hadn't had a hamburger since leaving Oklahoma and just looking at the sign made his mouth water.

He sat at a picnic table outside and tied Fan's reins around the bench leg. The mammoth twenty-five-cent hamburger tasted delicious; the ten-cent order of fries were crisp and hot, and the orange juice ice-cold. Jerry inhaled the food and had a refill of juice. A sign in the window advertised for a new employee. *Help Wanted, $.75/hr.* Jerry eyed it as he downed the last of his drink. *I'd give anything to work here for about a week and have all the hamburgers, fries, and orange juice I could hold.* Tethered close to the sidewalk, Fan caused a stir. Cars slowed and people gawked out their windows; kids on bicycles stopped. A little girl eating an apple walked past, accompanied by her mother. She turned around and, looking at Fan, asked Jerry if she could give her apple to "the pretty horse."

"Apples are Fan's favorite treat and I know for a fact she likes your calling her pretty." Jerry stood close and showed her how to protect her fingers while she fed Fan. Fan finished off the apple and delighted the little girl by nuzzling her hand for more. As darkness gathered, Jerry found a campsite a block north of the boulevard in San Dimas Canyon Park.

The next morning they got underway at sunup, about the time Foothill Boulevard began coming to life. One small town flowed into the next with no break in between. Not only were cars whizzing by in both directions on the two lanes of asphalt, but worse were buses spewing foul fumes. Though reasonable at first, the traffic seemed to double with each passing hour and by ten o'clock, Route 66 exploded with life on wheels. Stories in the newspapers back home claimed that new cars were impossible to obtain, and older cars at a premium. *Not in southern California,* Jerry thought. Thousands it seemed, raced back and forth; new cars, old cars, coupes, huge sedans and convertibles, many of them with white-wall tires. Jerry saw more cars with their tops down in the first three hours of June 21st than he'd seen in his entire life. Hair flying, people in convertibles laughing and talking, raced past them with radios blaring. Jerry heard snatches of songs he recognized. People honked and waved and shouted *hello!* He sat tall in the saddle, feeling a little like an alien.

Sunny and mild, the weather felt nothing like the overwhelming heat of the desert. Every street he passed, he caught sight of flowers, all of them blooming in profusion. There were giant shade trees, lush green lawns, and manicured grounds, so very different from the desert plants and parched landscape that Jerry had grown accustomed to seeing. In the city of Monrovia, Foothill Boulevard dissolved into a fusion of orange groves, fancy new developments, Spanish-styled mansions, and businesses. It seemed that every block had an office or public building with pink bougainvillea winding its way up a wall onto a red tile roof, leaving a trail of browned-tinged petals in its climb.

Two or three miles west of Monrovia, Jerry and Fan crossed into the bustling city of Pasadena and rode along Colorado Boulevard. Nestled at the base of the San Gabriel Mountains, the city retained the strong Spanish and Mexican influence of its early heritage; the structures built with thick walls, red tile roofs, and arched porticos that faced the street. Unlike the busy street they rode along, the neighborhoods adjacent to Colorado Boulevard appeared stately and serene. Jerry glanced down one broad street after another, amazed and impressed at the size of the rambling, Spanish-style mansions. Two and three stories tall, each built in different design but with similar materials, the effect very pleasing to the eye. Majestic sycamores and elms lined the streets, living symbols of the city's early beginnings. Gnarled limbs and broad green leaves embraced over the center of the streets blocking out the sun. Jerry had grown to love shade. His eyes sought out shade and he felt drawn toward it. Fan loved it, too. Though the temperature was mild, Jerry had a tug of war going with Fan, she trying to head for the shade of a front yard, and he attempting to rein her back onto noisy Colorado Boulevard.

Day forty-nine of his journey. Jerry had spent the majority of the last forty-eight days in wide open spaces with only the sky, the earth, and his horse for company. Here he saw no open space except for the few remaining remnants of orange orchards, most with *For Sale* signs on them. Every inch of ground had been claimed, dissected by fences and covered with houses, businesses, or public buildings, what remained covered by lawn, gravel, asphalt, or concrete. Even the mountains to the north had signs of development creeping up their slopes. Except for the distant mountain tops, Jerry could find no place for the eye to rest.

A city on the move, Pasadena was much larger to start with than Palm Springs. But like the desert city, Pasadena was in the midst of growth it could not contain. Again, Jerry saw no evidence of a shortage of building materials. Everywhere he looked he saw new construction: schools, housing tracts, highways, churches, and a huge shopping center with yet another sign *Future Home of Bullock's Department Store*. Surrounded by cars, traffic, confusion and noise, people on bicycles and motorcycles—a motorized frenzy—Jerry felt overwhelmed by the pace.

More than just agriculture disappearing, people scurrying about, or signs heralding the opening of a new school or department store, Pasadena projected a feeling; a sense that it would at any moment explode out of its boundaries—a gangly adolescent bursting out of his clothes before your very eyes. The pace wasn't the only harbinger of a new era.

The people were as well; the way they looked, the way they dressed. Men and women in shorts, men in short-sleeved shirts, and some men wore no shirt at all—never in Oklahoma! Jerry rode past tanned energetic-looking women, their short hair styled in finger-waves. And men with their hair Brylcreamed to perfection, all of them giving them quick smiles and curious looks. He caught bits of conversations: "Just got here from Iowa." "Enrolling in Caltech on the GI Bill." "Got a job at the Jet Propulsion Lab." "Just bought a new house." "Now that the war's over, I'm going to…"

The journey had lulled Jerry into an acceptance of solitude, of days on end with only Fan and a crackling campfire, or the prairie and a star-lit sky for company. All of a sudden he found himself smack in the middle of a world that was the antithesis of solitude, exactly what Jimmy Wakely described. Exciting and mind-boggling, it was nearly as overwhelming as the Mojave Desert's blinding sun. And compared to the quiet and solitude of the Bar R Ranch, southern California felt to Jerry like being on a different planet.

A sign announcing *Brookside Park, Turn Right One Mile,* couldn't have come at a better time. Fan needed a place to rest, to get out of the traffic and have some water and food. Jerry turned onto Rosemont Avenue for a mile and then west into the park. Fan headed for the first shade she saw, but Jerry noticed something a lot more impressive than shade. A stadium loomed upward out of the trees right in front of him.

"Wow!" was all he could say, gawking up at the edifice. "Fan, that's the Rose Bowl!"

The structure dwarfed the trees and surroundings. Massive round cement columns spaced evenly around the perimeter supported the oblong shaped stadium. Jerry dismounted and led Fan around the periphery, occasionally pausing to look up. Each time he stopped, Fan started to graze. "Sorry, girl, we'll stop soon as we walk all the way around." At the south end they encountered the main gate, signified by a large neon rose and underneath the words *Rose Bowl*. Friday noon, not a soul in sight, and the gates wide open—Jerry couldn't believe his eyes. He tentatively walked through the opening with Fan beside him. "Would you look at this, Fan," he whispered. "This is the most famous stadium in the country." They continued through the tunnel another thirty feet, Jerry craning his neck at the ceiling, the walls, and the dirt floor. When they reached the end of the tunnel, above the roof of the underground passage Jerry spied rows of seats divided into sections, each section at least fifty rows high.

"My gosh, Fan, this place must hold fifty thousand people." The thought occurred that ending up at the Rose Bowl like they did—totally by accident—could only happen once in a lifetime, and he wasn't about to miss it. The minute he climbed back on Fan, she started moving forward. "You must want to see this place, too." Fan and Jerry relished the tunnel's deep shade and then emerged into dazzling sunlight.

Poised at the top of a wide concrete ramp, Jerry noted that it sloped downward about seventy feet onto a dirt track that encircled the stadium. When his eyes adjusted to the bright light, he took in a full view of the Rose Bowl, a place he had only pictured while listening to football games on New Year's Day. The sight was beyond anything he'd ever imagined, but from his vantage point seventy feet above the stadium floor, the goal posts and hundred yards of grass appeared to be small-scale versions of the real thing. Something in the distance caught his eye; two horses harnessed to a cart stood at the far left-end of the track. Jerry shaded his eyes and squinted to make sure. "Trotters." A man on his knees was working on one of the cart's wheels.

Jerry urged Fan forward and let her make her way down the ramp onto the track. She immediately strained left, wanting to head toward the horses, but Jerry reined her to the right. "Come on, Fan, let's go the long way around so we can take in this whole place." Being down on the track, Jerry's perspective totally changed.

Everything now seemed gigantic; the endless rows of seats looked like they stretched into the clouds. Fan wanted to eat the lush grass but he held firm to her reins as he counted seventy rows in a section and more than twenty-five sections. From this vantage point, the stadium looked more like it held a hundred thousand people.

And the playing field, every line painted white, straight and perfect on the dark green grass, looked big enough to hold a battleship. Jerry had been to plenty of Guthrie High School football games and played on its field with his friends many times. He knew first-hand the length and width of an ordinary playing field. This field was anything but ordinary. This was the Rose Bowl—as grand as anything he had ever seen.

Jerry rode mid-way around and then reined Fan up and listened. *Quiet, so very quiet. No sound at all.* Down on the track away from the noise and traffic outside, the stadium was a world unto itself. Like the Palo Duro to the plains above it. "What must it be like to play football here, to win a game in front of a hundred thousand cheering people?" he whispered. Jerry closed his eyes.

Perhaps it was the result of being tired to the point of exhaustion. Or maybe it was acknowledging that he and Fan had cheated death, not once but how many times? It's possible that being in *the Rose Bowl,* the embodiment of California and their goal, or the accumulation of experiences hitting him all at once—or perhaps little of all three—Jerry didn't know. But he heard it as surely as he felt the sun on his face. Cheering faint at first, it started like a rumble then grew louder, coming from every direction. Then Jerry heard it full-blown, just like he'd heard it over the radio on New Year's Day. Only these cheers weren't coming from a radio, and they weren't for football players from Alabama or USC. A thrill raced across his shoulders and down his spine. Above the crowd noise, an announcer's booming voice reverberated throughout the stadium. *Ladies and gentlemen of the Rose Bowl. Let's hear it… for Jerry Van Meter and his horse, Fan……from Guthrieee……Oklahomahhh!*

Eyes closed, Jerry drank it in—a hundred thousand people screaming and yelling, raining down applause on an ordinary cowboy and his extraordinary horse. Every nerve tingled; a sensation of triumph detonated his weariness and exploded it into thousands of tiny fragments. Jerry straightened up and sat ramrod straight in the saddle, his heart hammering, and then raised his arms in victory. He caught his breath and held it—trying to forever stamp this moment in his memory. *We won, Fan. Dammitall, we won!*

Fan moved beneath him; Jerry exhaled and opened his eyes. *Poof,*
the crowd and the cheers were gone. All was eerily silent once more.
The feeling lingered for a moment as Jerry glanced around the empty
stadium and then scattered into the warm California air like leaves
caught in a breeze.

Fan, no longer able to ignore something good to eat, headed for the
lush grass on the field a few feet away. Jerry let her graze at the edge.
"If ever a horse deserved to eat someplace special, it's you." He only
let her eat a small amount because she pulled out the grass, roots and
all. Jerry dismounted and scuffed over the spot with his boot. He led
Fan back onto the track and walked in the direction of the trotters. He
put his hand on her neck. "What I want to know, Fan, does Rose Bowl
grass taste better?" All that her look told him was that she wanted
more.

Still bent down working on the cart, the man hadn't realized that
Jerry and Fan were on the floor of the stadium. When he heard them
approach, he stood up and turned around, a surprised look on his face.
"Who in the world are you?"

"Just a tired Oklahoma cowboy on his way to Hollywood."

The man's surprised look gave way to a smile. "Do you know
where you are?"

"Yup, the Rose Bowl, Granddaddy of 'em all." The man chuckled
as he offered his hand and then introduced himself as the Rose Bowl
caretaker.

When Jerry told him about their journey, the caretaker invited
them to rest a bit. "Do you think your horse could use some water and
hay?"

"Yes, sir, Fan can *always* use water and hay."

The caretaker broke open a bale and piled some hay on the edge of
the grass. "You look pretty worn out, might as well rest while your
horse has something to eat. This trip sounds interesting. I'd like to hear
more about it."

Jerry removed Fan's saddle and both of them smiled watching her roll like a puppy on the lush grass. Fan kept rubbing her head back and forth in the thick grass. "Now I can tell everybody, without lying, that the both of us made it into the end zone in the Rose Bowl." When Fan got up, she drank her fill and then moved to the pile of hay. Jerry stretched out on his side, head propped on his hand. The sun felt warm, the grass as thick and soft as a bed. He asked all kinds of questions about the Rose Bowl, about the stadium, the games played and the famous players who played in them. The caretaker knew it all. Hired during initial construction of the stadium, he was there for the first game in 1923, USC beating Penn State, fourteen to three. Twenty-three years later, he was now in charge of Rose Bowl maintenance.

The stadium seated 83,677 people, the approximate population of the city of Pasadena. The caretaker added that he'd heard talk that it might be enlarged in the next couple of years to one hundred thousand seats. Jerry asked if he had a favorite game and the caretaker nodded. "1942 when Oregon State hung on in a close game over Duke, twenty to sixteen. It wasn't a high-scoring game like I like, but for some reason we don't usually get those in this bowl. That was my favorite because you didn't know until the last minute whether Oregon State or Duke would pull it off. It was a memorable game. Did you hear the USC/Alabama game this year?"

"I did. Surprised me that USC got beat," Jerry said.

"Me, too," the caretaker said. "USC has played here more than any other school, nine times in the last twenty-three years, and up to that game they were undefeated. Those Alabama boys felt pretty proud of themselves."

Jerry thanked the caretaker for his kindness to Fan, who after finishing off the hay had fallen asleep. The soft grass and warm sun made it difficult for Jerry to get up and urge Fan to do the same. As he put her saddle back on, Jerry acknowledged that he would have liked to take a nap, too.

But Hollywood waited. The end of the journey was at hand.

– 33 –

End of the Journey

Daily Variety, June 21, 1946
• *Jerry Lewis Discovers Singer Dean Martin in Atlantic City* •
• *Elizabeth Taylor Shares Top Billing with Canine in The Courage Of Lassie* •
• *Newcomer Kirk Douglas, a Rising Star* •

The extremely heavy traffic they encountered after leaving the Rose Bowl, resulted in frustratingly slow progress. A Friday afternoon, it seemed as though everyone in Los Angeles had some-place to drive. At the western edge of Pasadena, Route 66 turned southwest aiming towards its final destination in Santa Monica. Jerry bid a silent goodbye to the famous highway as he and Fan continued west; their destination the southern edge of North Hollywood. They traveled on whatever street had the least amount of traffic, at times ending up in neighborhoods with children playing baseball. It was slow going.

Jerry had Kevin Lamb's note with Pete's address on it. Unfortunately, the verbal directions he gave had been vague: "Try to find Camarillo Street. Keep going until you get to a corner with this hacienda-looking house that has a pasture and a big barn. Turn right just past the barn. You can't miss it. Pete's place isn't too far, maybe five miles from there." Jerry tried to remember Kevin's instructions after the initial turn he said to take, but standing alongside his trailer at the time, Jerry grudgingly admitted that he remembered more about what Kevin said about date palms than his directions. The fact that their conversation took place only four hours after he'd walked in off the desert, it was a miracle he remembered anything at all.

Jerry found Camarillo Street around six p.m. and recognized the hacienda house with the pasture and barn. Turning right as instructed, he soon discovered the reason for Kevin's vague directions: this neighborhood of farms was in the midst of being gobbled up by the city. The area was a jumble of city lots, houses with adjoining pastures, and streets with no outlet. Making it worse, not all of the roads had signs and, on the ones that did, some of the names changed at an intersection or a bend in the road. Finally admitting he didn't remember any of what Kevin told him, Jerry began searching in what he considered a systematic pattern.

When that did not find Pete Wilson's house, he stopped and asked for assistance. The first gentleman he asked said he didn't recognize the address or Pete Wilson's name. Another helpful resident tried looking up Pete's name in his telephone book but found no listing. Jerry retraced his way through several streets. They had twenty minutes of sun left and, at most, an hour of daylight after that. He was beat and Fan had to be exhausted. He considered making camp in one of the pastures and starting his search the following morning, but tomorrow was Saturday, June 22, the fiftieth day. And Jerry remembered the promise he made to himself that he would beat the deadline. They were too close to quit; he damn-well intended to make it.

The last resident he asked had mentioned an area where he thought the ranch might be. "About two or three miles that way," he said, pointing to the northeast. "I kinda remember horse trailers going by here in that direction, but I've never been up there."

Jerry rode to the northernmost street, one he had already searched. But this time he turned east for another mile then tried two or three more streets—still nothing. Dread mounting, he directed Fan around a corner and east again onto a gravel road they had yet to try. They passed an orchard that ran along one side of the road, a pasture on the other. Then glancing ahead, Jerry spotted Pete's house—just as Kevin had described it. A mailbox at the edge of the road with the name "P. Wilson" confirmed their find. Jerry's heart skipped a beat at the sight.

The sun's last rays bathed the house in gold and pinks, a radiant sunset glinting off its windows. To Jerry, Pete's ranch represented the best that southern California had to offer, a lush green pasture, even a creek ambling across the property. It had trees of every shape and size. Fruit trees, towering sycamores, elms with huge trunks, tall airy trees with delicate leaves and purple flowers—more trees than Jerry had imagined at the height of his sun-baked fantasy. An arbor attached to the side of the house had grape vines intertwined through the lattice work, bunches of still-green grapes peeking through the spaces.

Jerry stared, wondering if this could be a fatigue-induced mirage for Pete's ranch had everything that he had promised Fan when he wasn't at all sure they would find their way out of the desert. The house was old like the ranch house at the Bar R, except this one had two stories, a steep roof with fancy gables, and looked to be considerably bigger.

Jerry sat atop Fan at the edge of the quiet road, trying to stamp the sight and this moment into his memory. The house, the shade trees and pasture symbolized their goal, the purpose and objective that had kept them going on what felt like an endless journey. It took a few minutes to sink in that they had made it. They were in Hollywood, that magical place he'd only heard about, fifteen hundred miles and another world away from the one he knew.

Images of the last forty-nine days raced through his head in a silent movie rendering of their journey, speeding to this instant, this road, this house, and the realization that the adventure was over. Jerry dismounted and stood holding Fan's reins, her head close to his. "I want you to remember this, girl. You did it. You're the one who got us here," he whispered. Excitement, danger, exhaustion, laughter, loneliness, and wonder—it was all over now. Triumph, pride, fear, accomplishment, and expectation—they would drive them no more. A release of breath held until the journey ended and now it had, a sharp, bittersweet moment.

Jerry led Fan across the grass toward the house. A spacious porch ran across the front. The door stood ajar, the opening covered by a wood framed screen that needed a touch of paint. When Jerry spotted chairs on the porch—comfortable old wooden chairs with cane bottoms and scuffed legs—he knew he would like this fellow Pete Wilson. Jerry knocked.

"Hold on a minute," a booming voice sounded from somewhere inside. Jerry stepped back off the porch and stood near Fan. A lanky silhouette appeared in the shadows and approached the screen. Pete Wilson came out of the house, his expression changing from curious to alarm. "What in the world, cowboy? You look like you—"

"We just rode in from Oklahoma." Jerry handed him the note from Kevin.

Pete wasted no time; he led the exhausted pair to the barn and helped Jerry tend to Fan. Jerry quickly discovered he was an expert horseman by the way he checked Fan over and from the supply of medicines and ointments he kept in the barn. With his eyes closed, Pete ran his hands over her withers and chest and down her legs. "Lost quite a bit of weight, haven't you, girl." He talked and worked like a vet; it was obvious he had done this a thousand times. While they tended her, Jerry told him about meeting Kevin in Indio and briefly about their journey. When Pete replied, "Well, I'll be damned," exactly like Kevin, Jerry had his first laugh.

About six feet tall, Pete Wilson was an imposing man; it showed in his carriage and his obvious strength. Lean, spare, and broad-shouldered, he had gun-metal gray hair tinged with silver around his weathered face. Whether he was widowed, divorced, or never married, he didn't mention, saying only that he lived alone. He called this twenty acres home, the place where he trained and housed his best trick horses, though he told Jerry that he had another, larger ranch in Frazier Park in the hills north of Los Angeles.

After Pete reassured him that Fan was suffering mainly from exhaustion and dehydration, and that he felt she would improve with time and care, Jerry allowed himself to relax. Fan would get what Jerry had promised her: a clean stall near other horses and plenty of cool water, hay, and rolled oats. "She'll be okay, but what she needs now more than anything is rest," Pete said. As he led the way to the house, Jerry asked Pete if he could use the telephone.

Pete pointed to the phone in the living room. They took a swing through the kitchen and Pete motioned to the icebox. "Help yourself after you make your calls. This is your home as long as you would like to stay. I want to hear your whole story from the beginning over coffee or whenever you feel like waking up in the morning." He showed Jerry an upstairs bedroom, then pointed out the bathroom down the hall and handed him some towels. "I expect you to make a dent in that food in the icebox. Make yourself at home and I'll see you whenever you're good and rested. We wrapped up a film today and I don't have to work tomorrow, so we can do whatever you'd like. Maybe you'd like to see a little of Hollywood."

"I really appreciate your taking us in, it sure is ni—"

"It gets lonesome around here. I'm happy to have the company and a real Oklahoma cowboy, at that." Pete said goodnight and disappeared into his room at the other end of the hall.

Jerry first called his parents in Guthrie. With a two-hour time difference, it was ten-thirty in Oklahoma, nearing his parents' bedtime. They would be in the living room reading and listening to music on the radio, and his brothers were most likely already asleep in the bunkhouse. The phone rang three times before he heard his mother's voice. Jerry's heart quickened as the operator asked her if she would accept the charges for a long distance call from a Jerry Van Meter in Hollywood, California.

"Most certainly," came her firm reply. He heard her calling his father. "Vearl, come quick, it's Jerry!"

He spilled out his news in one breath. "I made it, Mom. I'm in Hollywood. We did it in forty-nine days. We won!"

"Jerry, I am thrilled! And so proud of you, son, are you okay? You sound exhausted." Jerry assured her he felt fine, *really* tired, but otherwise fine. "My, my, it's hard to imagine you being in Hollywood, California. That is so far away."

Jerry asked about his brothers, and then his father got on the phone. Vearl sounded relieved and genuinely happy to hear from him. He asked Jerry if the desert had been tough. Jerry promised to tell him all about it if he would make him a big bowl of fresh peach ice cream when he returned. That brought laughter—an unusual response for his father. "I'll take you up on that. Congratulations, son. What you did is a big accomplishment. You should be very proud. We are." The respect that came through in his father's voice and his compliment made Jerry take a deep breath. He closed his eyes, allowing a new vision of himself to emerge as he listened. Their brief conversation melted away a lifetime of father-son tension between two very different individuals.

Jerry made his second call to Frank Eaton's place in Perkins. His mother had said Rolla and Frank were visiting there for a few days. Frank's daughter, Orpha, answered the phone. She accepted the charges then called her father. It took a few minutes for Frank to understand that it was Jerry on the phone, calling from Hollywood. Frank sounded half-asleep. "Is this Jerry?"

"It's me, Frank. Sounds like I woke you up."

"I mighta been noddin' off in my chair. Did I hear right? Did Orpha say you was callin' from Hollywood?"

"Dammitall, I sure am. We made it, Frank!"

Jerry had to hold the phone away from his ear. Frank started whooping and hollering, then yelled at Rolla. "Rolla! Get your sorry hide over here. I got a *real* cowboy on the line." Frank bombarded Jerry with questions, not waiting to hear the answer before asking another. "Hold on a minute, Jerry. Your grandpa is slower 'n molasses in January." Frank turned away from the phone. "For goodness sakes, Rolla, put a little pepper in your step."

Jerry expected to hear his grandfather's voice. Instead he heard Rolla and Frank laughing and talking with Orpha. Finally, Rolla came on the phone, shouting as always. "I knew right from the beginning you'd do it. I am proud of you, Jerry. I just wish Charlie Goodnight could be here. He'd be proud as a peacock, too, son."

"You never told me how much you'd win if I won, but from the sounds of it, it must be a lot." Jerry shook with silent laughter as the reactions came in. The full realization began to dawn what he and Fan had accomplished—and it felt good.

"I'm not hollering about the money. That ain't worth a tinker's damn. You proving what a real cowboy can do is what is we're excited about. You done more than me 'n Frank ever did."

"What do you mean? I thought this was the same as the two of you riding the Goodnight-Loving Trail, except for a herd."

"Frank 'n me been talkin' about that." Rolla suddenly sounded serious. "With Jimmy going on like he did, I guess I got carried away. When I made that bet, I didn't stop to think about us having a remuda. Our horses got to rest, and we had a bunch of cowhands to back us up if we got in trouble. You and Fan did it all by yourselves...by the way, is she okay?"

"She's real tired, but Fan is going to be fine, Grandpa." Never in his twenty years had Jerry heard his grandfather as excited or happy, or as talkative. Rolla recited Jimmy Wakely's phone number at his ranch in the San Fernando Valley and insisted Jerry call him immediately.

"Make sure to have Jimmy call me here at Frank's, soon as you finish talkin' to him. I got a little braggin' to do." Frank shouted good-bye from the background before Rolla hung up.

By the time Jerry dialed Jimmy's number, the enormity of their trip was beginning to sink in. A little girl identifying herself as Lindalee answered the phone. "Just a minute," she said and he heard her put the phone down, her young voice becoming distant. "Daddy, a man from Oklahoma, says his name is Jerry...something. He wants to talk to you."

Jerry recognized Jimmy's voice. "I'll just bet you do, Jerry Van Meter." He chuckled. "You calling me from someplace in Arizona to come and pick you up?"

Now Jerry laughed. "No. I'm happy to say I am practically in your back yard. Sorry to call so late, but I just hung up from talking to Grandpa. He insisted I call you right now and let you know I made it. You're supposed to call him as soon as we finish. I'll warn you, you're in for some bragging." Jerry gave Jimmy the Perkins phone number.

"I've always admired Rolla, liked him even when he's cantankerous. Your granddad won the bet fair and square, so I'll just have to listen to him brag." Jimmy sounded genuinely pleased. "How about coming out to the ranch tomorrow? I want to hear all about your ride, and I'd like you to meet Inez and the kids."

"I'm staying here in Hollywood with Pete Wilson, the head stunt man for Republic Pictures. He said he just wrapped up a picture today. I'll see if maybe he could drive me up to your place tomorrow."

"Make it in the afternoon and plan on staying for supper. Inez will treat you to some good home cooking. I'd like to meet Pete Wilson. I've heard about him from Wayne Burson, my stunt double. Wayne says he's one of the best."

"I'll check with him in the morning and let you know. You can give us directions then."

"I just want you to know, Jerry, that I didn't believe *anybody* could make that ride in fifty days. But Rolla said you could. Frank, too. Your grandfather never doubted you for a minute. He has every right to be proud, and so should you. You are a cowboy clean through just like he said. And that Goodnight tradition? I'll tell Rolla not to worry. It's in fine shape."

Jerry hung up and sat in the darkened room, allowing Jimmy's words to register. How embarrassed he remembered feeling, seeing him that evening after the parade. *Trying to avoid any mention of the navy or myself.* That evening seemed a lifetime ago.

Following Pete's instructions, Jerry made himself a huge sandwich from fixings he found in the icebox. He had his first hot shower in forty-nine days, with real shampoo and good-smelling soap. By the time he crawled into bed, fatigue had triumphed; he could no longer keep his eyes open. When Jerry stretched out and weariness enveloped him; it did so on a comfortable mattress with clean sheets and a soft pillow. *Oh, how good this feels.* Before he could surrender to sleep, Jerry kept the last promise he'd made to himself. "Thank you, Lord, for making this trip with me and Fan. It turned out to be the hard way, but thanks to you, we made it alri…"

Sleep captured the last of the cowboy's prayer.

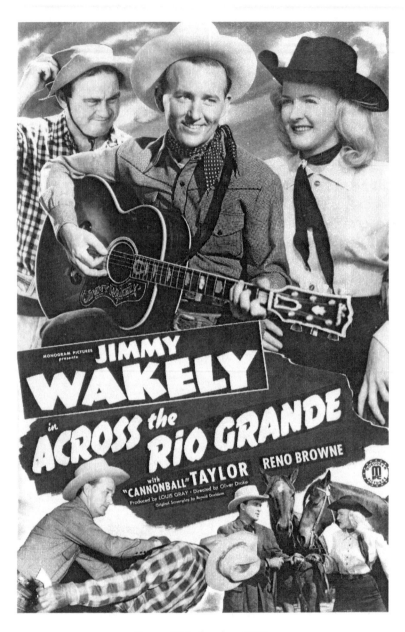

Jimmy Wakely, circa 1945.
Photo courtesy of Lindalee Wakely

Epilogue

Pete Wilson took Jerry in without a moment's hesitation, opening his heart and home to a fellow cowboy, one of his own kind. After a day of rest, Pete drove him north to San Fernando Valley in response to Jimmy Wakely's invitation to visit his ranch. After greeting them, Wakely said he didn't get the chance to call Rolla the previous evening like he promised, "because your Granddad called me first and he and Frank did some serious braggin'." He relayed their lively conversation but made no mention of the bet.

After giving Jerry and Pete a tour of his ranch, Wakely told Jerry the reason he accepted Rolla's bet. "I didn't believe for a minute that *any* cowboy could do what you did." Pete agreed and added that Fan "was a remarkable horse." As they finished the tour, Jerry had to smile listening to Wakely and Wilson discussing Republic and Monogram movies, and trading names of actors they had worked with.

Thirty-two-year-old Jimmy Wakely had already been Monogram Pictures' singing-cowboy star for six years with a dozen B movies to his credit. Labeled the Bing Crosby of country western music, Wakely also enjoyed a thriving singing career, traveling and performing at county fairs and western events. One of those events was the 52nd Annual Cherokee Strip Celebration in Enid, Oklahoma where he met up with old friends Rolla Goodnight and Frank "Pistol Pete" Eaton, the meeting that led to their bet.

On the drive back, Pete Wilson told Jerry that in Hollywood, Wakely was indeed thought of as a "genuine movie star." And after hearing their comments about his ride, Jerry left the ranch with a new appreciation for his accomplishment. As soon as Pete gave his okay that Fan was well enough to travel, he and Jerry trailered the exhausted mare up to his ranch in the hills north of Los Angeles. Pete said that his sixty-acre property was where he stabled the rest of his horses until he needed them for a movie. He asked his caretaker to give Fan special care and attention and, after hearing Jerry's story, the man promised he most certainly would.

Later the following week, Pete took a rested Jerry with him to Republic Pictures Studios in Hollywood. They hired Jerry on the spot as a wrangler in their western B movies, his job riding broncs and driving runaway stage coaches and covered wagons. It was an exciting time for Jerry, getting to watch famous movie stars at work. Pete made sure to let him know when Republic's big name cowboy stars were filming.

Jerry got to watch Gene Autry riding Champion on the studio's famous back lot, an expansive grass-covered parcel with the L.A. River twisting through it. During the filming of *Sioux City Sue,* starring Autry, Pete treated Jerry to a stroll down Western Street, the make-believe dirt avenue lined with old-west facades and wooden boardwalks. Always gracious, he also introduced Jerry to Republic cowboy star Monte Hale whom Pete had worked with earlier in 1946 on the movie *Home on the Range.*

After working for a month at Republic, Jerry concluded that movie cowboyin' was nothing like the real thing. During those four weeks Pete received frequent reports from Fan's caretaker that she was steadily improving. The mare spent her month of R&R running free on the sixty-acre ranch and when Jerry saw her again, the change was remarkable. Fan had gained back much of her weight and to his relief, acted like her former feisty self. Pete agreed that she had improved enough to take her back to his ranch in Hollywood to continue her recovery. Every moment he wasn't at work, Jerry lavished care and attention on Fan, making sure to fulfill his promise to her in the desert; plenty of shade, fresh water, and all the feed and timothy hay she wanted. Jerry and Pete watched Fan return to health, enjoying the companionship of other horses, and receiving what she loved most—attention.

While Jerry was away at Republic Studios, one of Pete's neighbors, Sarah, a girl of fourteen on her summer vacation from school, began visiting Fan. Soon, her sporadic visits turned to daily visits, Fan trotting up to her expectantly for the treat she brought. Jerry caught glimpses of Sarah stroking Fan as she talked to her, and it tugged at his heart to see Fan follow her around like a puppy. *Like she used to do with me.* Not long after, it became a pattern for Sarah to arrive before Jerry and Pete left for work each morning and often still be there when they returned home.

Fan seemed to revel in the girl's affection. Sarah lavished attention on the mare, feeding her oats and her favorite treats and grooming Fan until she sparkled like a star show horse. As the weeks passed, Sarah taught Fan tricks and then began riding her around the grounds of Pete's ranch. The affection between them flourished until Jerry could not ignore the bond developing between them. Their closeness created conflicting feelings, distress at being replaced, but on the other hand gratitude at Fan getting the attention she craved.

An accomplished rider, the girl told Jerry that her dream was to become a trick rider, riding in rodeos, western shows, and county fairs. She and her father had been looking for a steady horse for two years; one that would be responsive and loving, not skittish. She wanted a strong unflappable horse, "just like Fan." At summer's end, Fan's new friend told Jerry, shyly, that she had fallen in love with his beloved Osage Indian mare. A visit from the girl's father reinforced Sarah's story and the fact that he would like to buy Fan for his daughter. "I give you my word that Fan will receive the very best of care. She will be treated like a queen."

Jerry stayed with Pete at his North Hollywood home for five and a half months and worked at Republic Pictures until a long-simmering strike erupted into violence. After months of failed negotiations and escalating clashes that dominated nationwide newspaper and radio news, the conflict came to a head in December 1946. The tension between the splintered unions and studios reached an impasse that brought film production in Hollywood to a halt.

Pete invited Jerry to wait out the strike, assuring him he was welcome to stay and return to work at Republic when the strike ended. But deep down, Jerry knew the time had come for him to go home. The return trip to Oklahoma by train would be difficult on Fan, but even more importantly, the life awaiting her there would never be what he knew this special horse deserved. Not only did Sarah give Fan the affection and constant attention she craved, the young girl had already shown that Fan would receive care befitting a royal breed. Sarah and her family offered everything Jerry desperately wanted but could not give to his beloved Osage Indian mare.

He sold Fan to the young girl in December 1946, shortly before boarding a train for Oklahoma, an act of unselfish love and a heart-breaking moment. Jerry loved Fan. "The best horse I've ever known," he told me during our first interview. He never saw or heard of Fan again, a fact I found difficult to grasp at first, having come to know just how much he loved her. Perhaps it was the pain that came through in his voice, or the wistful look I detected when Jerry spoke of Fan, but I did not ask him why he didn't keep in touch with Sarah about his beloved horse. Sometimes when a reader brings up the question "why didn't he?" I am unable to offer a concrete explanation. But upon reflection, given the opportunity to ask him today, I would do the same thing. What he did was an act of love so unselfish, so painful, that no explanation is adequate. The answer speaks to the very heart and soul of Jerry Van Meter, the man who vowed that either his beloved horse would walk out of the Mojave Desert with him or he would stay with her until the end.

Jerry and Fan shared an amazing experience, riding fifteen hundred miles to win a bet, to prove a point, to honor tradition. An experience shared by cowboys of old? Possibly. Duplicated in the post-war era? Not that this author is aware.

Jimmy Wakely paid off the bet to Rolla, the amount of which they took to their graves. Rolla Goodnight and Frank "Pistol Pete" Eaton, proud symbols of the era they personified, kept cowboyin' together almost to the end. Frank lived to be ninety-eight and died at his home in Perkins, Oklahoma on April 8, 1958. Devastated by the loss of his friend of seventy-six years, Rolla survived another fourteen months; he died in Guthrie on January 8, 1960 at age eighty-nine. Jimmy Wakely, who experienced a successful singing career after his movie career ended, died at age sixty-eight in 1982 in Mission Hills, California.

Jerry left Hollywood and returned to cowboyin' in Oklahoma, but only for a short time. A first marriage with four children born in quick succession followed, bringing the need to earn more money. He turned to mining in New Mexico, Colorado, and later on to mines in a half-dozen other western states, all which paid significantly more than being a ranch foreman. About the marriage, which eventually ended, Jerry was hesitant to speak except to say that the years that followed were very difficult.

In the mid-seventies while mining near Lyman, Wyoming, by happenstance, Jerry met elementary school teacher, Hazel Joyce, "a red-haired, dynamite of a woman," he said, and it was love at first sight. One issue, Hazel had seven children and he had four! When they married on March 25, 1978 and combined their families, Jerry joked that he now had his own football team. A few years after they were married, Jerry suffered a serious fall in the Laramie mine, his injuries significant enough to force him to retire from the dangerous profession.

He and Hazel settled in Kalispell, Montana and, surrounded by the majority of their children, the two enjoyed a happy, adventure-filled twenty years together. Their eleven children gave them twenty-six grandchildren, and at last count, six great-grandchildren. Hazel passed away at home in Kalispell on February 14, 1999.

Jerry and I remained close during the eight years I lived in Idaho; ours resembled a surrogate-father/daughter relationship. After I moved back to California in 2007, we kept in touch occasionally via telephone but, predictably, our communication declined over time. Still, as I did every year on his birthday, I phoned Jerry on February 13, 2009, his eighty-third birthday. We had a wonderful visit, talking about our fun-filled book tour, which because of our sizable entourage, Jerry described as "taking Oklahoma without firing a shot." Accompanying the two of us were three of his brothers and their wives, Jerry's stepdaughter, my husband, my two sisters, and one brother-in-law—thirteen in all. Jerry and I had two jam-packed weeks of appearances and book signings in six Oklahoma cities, and at each event Jerry was "the star." People waited in line to meet "the cowboy," shake his hand, and get Jerry's autograph in their book. An honor for both of us, Jerry and I rode in the 102nd Cherokee Strip parade in Enid—the same parade in which Rolla, Frank, and Jimmy Wakely rode, and led to the bet.

Jerry and I reminisced over our four-year struggle to take his adventure from interviews to our first book signing. Of note here, and for reasons I cannot explain so therefore attribute to Providence, fate, or karma, our first book signing took place on September 19, 1999 at the *Full Circle Bookstore* in Oklahoma City, exactly five years to the day that I first heard Jerry's story in the cowboy bar, and four years to the day from our very first interview—full circle indeed!

When it came time to say goodbye, Jerry and I ended our phone conversation as we had done a hundred times in our four years working together. I told him "I love you, cowboy," and he replied, "I love you, too, kid." Two months later on April 13, 2009, he died peacefully in his sleep. The eulogy I wrote about Jerry, a man I am deeply honored and privileged to have known, was read at the funeral in Kalispell by his brother, Jim Van Meter.

Jerry's adventure, "the great American cowboy rides again," proved something to Jimmy Wakely, an astute Hollywood movie star and part of the coming tide; and to Rolla Goodnight and Frank "Pistol Pete" Eaton, crusty old cowboys belonging to the age it replaced. By his journey Jerry demonstrated the adage: "courage is not the absence of fear but the conquest of it," and in doing so, proved that an ordinary young man and an extraordinary horse can lift themselves above the crowd and accomplish a remarkable feat.

In 1946, the United States was stirring and thumping its chest in celebration after four years of waiting and holding its breath while the world's eyes and ears were on Europe and the Pacific. A pivotal decade in America, the forties came to a close witnessing the largest spurt in births in U.S. history—the baby boomers—and the promise of a dazzling future.

Hollywood after the war, exploded with an influx of soldiers and sailors, truck drivers, cowboys, secretaries and clerks, all swept up in a make-believe world. Nothing more than kids, they came from large cities and small towns, from mundane jobs that suddenly seemed stifling. Hollywood became a magnet for young, beautiful people determined to succeed. They banded together and energized a magic city that promised money, freedom, and fame. The names and films of those *kids,* whose tenacity and talent persevered, are part and parcel of our culture. America's sudden new role as world leader propelled the country and its citizens along in a fast-paced tide of exciting discoveries and social progress. In that context, Jerry's adventure represents a step back in time, reminiscent of the nineteenth century. His was a personal quest that tested limits, nerve, and heart, the only reward words of praise, his memories, and a feeling of accomplishment.

From a twenty-first century perspective, Jerry's journey speaks not merely of a young man's commitment to honor two men he loved and revered, but even more it chronicled the end of an era in our country never again to be repeated—that door in our history is closed. Our next door to open did so to an era moving at warp-speed, bringing with it new values, new definitions, and technological change seemingly without limit.

Still, after more than sixty years of unparalleled progress, we continue to search out those special men and women upon whom an indefinable light shines—individuals we call heroes. The young cowboy from Oklahoma shared a brief moment in the make-believe world of Hollywood and then returned to the world he knew.

Jerry Van Meter started the adventure a confident boy of barely twenty. The journey, its travails and triumphs, produced a courageous and humble man, and an amazing story this author is proud to have told.

About the Author

PATTI DICKINSON, award winning author of the nonfiction *Coach Tommy Thompson & the Boys of Sequoyah*, and her newly released political thriller, *The Indian's Daughter*, is a native Oklahoman with Cherokee ancestry, and lives on the Central Coast of California. She has been a member of The Authors Guild since 1998.

Visit Patti at her website: www.pattianndickinson.org

CPSIA information can be obtained
at www.ICGtesting.com
Printed in the USA
FSOW01n0956250116
15995FS

CPSIA information can be obtained
at www.ICGtesting.com
Printed in the USA
FSOW01n0956250116
15995FS